Bake Sale Favorites

Publications International, Ltd.

Bake Sale Favorites

Introduction   6

Cookie Jar Favorites   12

Outrageous Brownies & Bars   26

Spectacular Cakes   40

Tantalizing Pies   56

Homemade Quick Breads   66

Quick Tricks with Mixes   80

Acknowledgments   91

Index   92

Introduction

Everyone loves a bake sale! It's the perfect time to bake your favorite treats, share them with friends and neighbors *and* raise money for a good cause. The hard part is deciding what to bake. You'll find plenty of ideas in *Bake Sale Favorites*—from fabulous cookies and brownies to irresistible pies, cakes and breads. Need a quick no-bake cookie? The world's easiest brownies? An old-fashioned cherry pie? They're all here in one jam-packed book! We've even included a chapter of quick recipes that start with mixes in case you're short on time. To ensure that your baked goods look as great as they taste, lots of baking and decorating tips as well as ideas for eye-catching displays and beautiful wrappings have been included. There's also plenty of information about storing and freezing so you can bake ahead or save extras for another time. So begin now to discover just how easy it is to have the most successful bake sale ever!

Baking Basics

• Read the entire recipe before you begin to be sure you have all the necessary ingredients and utensils.

• Remove butter, margarine and cream cheese from the refrigerator to soften, if necessary.

• Adjust oven racks and preheat the oven. Check oven temperature with an oven thermometer to make sure the temperature is accurate.

• Toast and chop nuts and melt butter and chocolate before preparing batter or dough.

• Always use the pan size suggested in the recipe. Prepare pans as directed.

• Choose cookie sheets that fit in your oven with at least 1 inch on all sides between the edge of the sheet and the oven wall.

• Grease cookie sheets only when the recipe recommends it; otherwise, the cookies may spread too much.

• Measure the ingredients accurately and assemble them in the order they are listed in the recipe.

• When baking more than one sheet of cookies at a time, it's best to rotate them for even baking. Halfway through the baking time, rotate the cookie sheets from front to back as well as from the top rack to the bottom rack.

• Always check for doneness at the minimum baking time given in the recipe.

Melting Chocolate

There are several methods for melting chocolate. They all begin with utensils that are completely dry. Moisture, whether from utensils or an accidental drop of water, causes chocolate to "seize," which means it becomes stiff and grainy. If this happens, try adding a ½ teaspoon of shortening (not butter or margarine, which contain water) for each ounce of chocolate and stir until smooth. When melting chocolate, avoid high heat as well as moisture, because chocolate scorches easily and once scorched cannot be used. Follow one of these three methods for successful melting.

Double Boiler: This is the safest method because it prevents scorching. Place the chocolate in the top of a double boiler or in a heatproof bowl over hot, not boiling, water; stir until smooth. (Make sure that the water remains just below a simmer and is 1 inch below the bottom of the top pan.) Be careful that no steam or water gets into the chocolate.

Direct Heat: Place the chocolate in a *heavy* saucepan and melt over *very* low heat, stirring constantly. Remove the chocolate from the heat as soon as it is melted. Be sure to watch the chocolate carefully because it scorches easily when using this method.

Microwave Oven: Place an unwrapped 1-ounce square or 1 cup of chocolate chips in a small microwavable bowl. Microwave on HIGH 1 to 1½ minutes, stirring after 1 minute. Be sure to stir microwaved chocolate since it may retain its original shape even when melted. It will taste burnt if microwaved after it has melted. Chocolate can also be melted in a small heavy resealable plastic food storage bag, turning the bag over after microwaving 1 minute. When the chocolate is melted, knead the bag until chocolate is smooth. Cut off a tiny corner of the bag and gently squeeze the bag to drizzle the chocolate.

Special Touches: Decorating

Great-looking baked goods go a long way toward making a bake sale successful. A few extra minutes spent on decorating can make all the difference. Try any of the following ideas to jazz up your cakes, cookies and pies. Also, look for "Make It Special" tips scattered throughout this publication.

Chocolate Drizzle: Melted chocolate or white chocolate provides an easy finish for many baked goods. Simply drizzle melted chocolate with a spoon or fork over baked goods or dip half of each cookie in melted chocolate. The contrast of a white chocolate drizzle on a brown chocolate cookie is sure to draw attention.

Chocolate Leaves: Chocolate leaves provide a sensational garnish for a layer cake. Melt chocolate as directed on page 7 except add 1 teaspoon shortening (not butter or margarine) for every 2 ounces of chocolate. Brush the underside of

clean, dry, nontoxic leaves, such as lemon, rose or camellia, with melted chocolate until the leaves are thickly and evenly coated. Wipe off any excess chocolate from the front of the leaves. Place leaves, chocolate side up, on waxed paper; let them stand in a cool, dry place until firm. *(Do not refrigerate.)* When chocolate is firm, carefully grasp the stems and peel leaves away from chocolate. Use immediately or chill until ready to use.

Chocolate Curls: This elegant and impressive garnish is the perfect topping for layer cakes. Melt chocolate as directed on page 7 except add 1 teaspoon shortening (not butter or margarine) for every 2 ounces of chocolate. Cool melted chocolate slightly; pour chocolate onto the back of a jelly-roll pan. Quickly spread it into a thin layer with a flat metal spatula. Let stand in a cool, dry place until the chocolate is firm. *(Do not*

refrigerate.) When chocolate is just firm, hold an offset metal spatula at a 45° angle and scrape chocolate into curls. Use a small skewer or wooden toothpick to transfer curls to waxed paper; store curls in a cool, dry place or use immediately.

Chocolate-Dipped Strawberries:
Turn an ordinary cake into a
spectacular one with two or three
chocolate-dipped strawberries. Or,
sell large strawberries dipped in
semisweet or white chocolate. Melt
chocolate as directed on page 7
(without shortening). Dip clean, dry
strawberries into melted chocolate

 until the
chocolate
covers about
two thirds
of the
strawberries.
Allow any
excess
chocolate to
drip off. Transfer strawberries to
waxed paper. Let stand in a cool,
dry place until chocolate is firm.
After the chocolate coating is firm,
the strawberries may be stored in
the refrigerator.

Powdered Sugar Glaze: A simple
glaze drizzled or spread on quick
breads, coffee cakes or other baked
goods is an attractive and easy
topping. Combine 1 cup sifted
powdered sugar and 5 teaspoons
milk in a small bowl. Add ½
teaspoon vanilla extract or other
flavoring, if desired. Stir until
smooth. If the glaze is too thin,
stir in additional powdered sugar;
if the consistency is too thick, add
additional milk, ½ teaspoon at a
time.

Toasting Nuts: Chopped nuts
make a great topping on frosted
treats. Toasting nuts intensifies their
flavor and fragrance. To toast nuts,
spread them in a single layer on a
cookie sheet. Bake in a preheated
325°F oven for 8 to 10 minutes or
until golden, stirring occasionally
to ensure even toasting. The nuts
will darken and become crisper as
they cool. To toast a small amount
of nuts, place them in a dry skillet
over low heat. Stir constantly for
2 to 4 minutes or until the nuts
darken slightly and become
fragrant. Always cool nuts before
using.

Toasting Coconut: Coconut
sprinkled on frosted cakes,
brownies and cookies adds a
distinctive appearance and flavor.
To toast coconut, spread a thin
layer of flaked coconut on a cookie
sheet. Bake in a preheated 325°F
oven for 7 to 10 minutes. Shake
the pan or stir the coconut
occasionally during baking to
promote even browning and prevent
burning.

Tinting Coconut: Tinted coconut
is a festive finish for cupcakes. To
tint coconut, simply dilute a few
drops of liquid food coloring with
½ teaspoon milk or water in a small
bowl. Add 1 to 1⅓ cups flaked
coconut and toss with a fork until
coconut is evenly tinted.

Special Touches: Packaging and Display

Cakes, pies and coffee cakes can be sold either whole or by the piece. Cookies, brownies, bars and muffins can be packaged by the dozen or individually. Or, allow buyers to create their own assortments. Offer some treats already wrapped in clear or tinted plastic wrap and tied with ribbon or raffia. Attractive displays help sell goods. Dress up the sale table with a colorful piece of fabric or an inexpensive tablecloth. Display the most stunning cakes, pies and cheesecakes by elevating them; pack cookies, brownies or muffins in decorative tins and boxes. Baskets lined with brightly colored cloth napkins will hold loads of individually wrapped goodies. Include your recipe complete with any special storage tips for an extra special touch. Look for additional "Sell It" tips throughout this publication.

Storing and Freezing

Since bake sales don't always happen at the most convenient times, plan ahead. Many items can be baked ahead and frozen; a variety of unbaked doughs can also be frozen to be baked up hot and fresh at the last minute. Not all baked goods are ideal for freezing, however; choose carefully before you begin baking.

Cookies & Bars: Unbaked cookie dough can be refrigerated for up to one week or frozen for up to six weeks. Rolls of dough (for slice-and-bake cookies) should be sealed tightly in plastic wrap; other doughs should be stored in airtight containers. For convenience, label plastic wrap or container with baking information.

Store soft and crisp cookies separately at room temperature to prevent changes in texture and flavor. Keep soft cookies in airtight containers. If they begin to dry out, add a piece of apple or a slice of bread to the container to help them retain moisture. Store crisp cookies in containers with loose-fitting lids to prevent moisture buildup. If the cookies become soggy, heat the undecorated ones in a 300°F oven for 3 to 5 minutes to restore crispness. Store cookies with sticky glazes, fragile decorations and icings in single layers between sheets of waxed paper.

As a rule, crisp cookies freeze better than soft, moist cookies. Rich, buttery bar cookies are an exception because they freeze extremely well. Freeze baked cookies in airtight containers or freezer bags for up to six months. Thaw cookies and brownies unwrapped at room temperature. Meringue-based cookies do not freeze well and chocolate-dipped cookies will discolor if frozen.

Cakes: Store one-layer frosted cakes in their baking pans, tightly covered. Store layered frosted cakes under a cake cover or under a large inverted bowl. Cakes with whipped cream frostings or cream fillings should be stored in the refrigerator. Unfrosted cakes can be frozen for up to four months if well-wrapped in plastic; thaw them, unwrapped, at room temperature. Frosted cakes should be frozen unwrapped until the frosting hardens, and then wrapped, sealed and frozen for up to two months. To thaw, remove the wrapping and thaw at room temperature or in the refrigerator. Cakes with fruit or custard fillings do not freeze well because they become soggy when thawed.

Pies: Unbaked pie dough can be frozen for later use. Simply flatten the dough into disks and stack them in a freezer bag with waxed paper separating the layers. Freeze prepared pastry shells in pie pans with waxed paper between the shells. Disks of pie dough must be thawed before using them whereas pastry shells should be baked frozen.

Meringue-topped pies are best when served the day they are made; leftovers should be refrigerated. Custard or cream pies should be refrigerated immediately after cooling. Fruit pies should be covered and stored at room temperature overnight; refrigerate them for longer storage.

To freeze unbaked fruit pies, do not cut steam vents in the top crust. Cover them with inverted paper plates for extra protection and package in freezer bags or plastic wrap. To bake, do not thaw. Cut slits in the top crust and allow an additional 15 to 20 minutes of baking time. Baked fruit pies can be frozen after they're completely cooled. To serve, let the pie thaw at room temperature for two hours, then heat until warm. Pies with cream or custard fillings and meringue toppings do not freeze well.

Breads & Muffins: Quick breads should be wrapped well in plastic wrap and stored at room temperature to stay fresh up to one week. Or, they may be frozen for up to three months wrapped in heavy-duty foil. Muffins should be stored in a sealed plastic food storage bag up to three days. Or, they may be frozen for up to one month wrapped in heavy-duty foil.

Cookie Jar Favorites

Raspberry Pecan Thumbprints

2 cups all-purpose flour
1 cup pecan pieces, finely
    chopped, divided
½ teaspoon ground cinnamon
¼ teaspoon ground allspice
⅛ teaspoon salt
1 cup (2 sticks) butter, softened
½ cup packed light brown sugar
2 teaspoons vanilla
¼ cup seedless raspberry jam

Preheat oven to 350°F. Combine flour, ½ cup pecans, cinnamon, allspice and salt in medium bowl. Beat butter in large bowl with electric mixer at medium speed until smooth. Gradually beat in sugar; increase speed to high and beat until light and fluffy. Beat in vanilla until blended. Beat in flour mixture at low speed just until blended.

Form dough into 1-inch balls; flatten slightly and place on ungreased cookie sheets. Press down with thumb in center of each ball to form indentation. Pinch together any cracks in dough. Fill each indentation with generous ¼ teaspoon jam. Sprinkle filled cookies with remaining ½ cup pecans.

Bake 14 minutes or until just set. Let cookies stand on cookie sheets 5 minutes; transfer to wire racks to cool completely. Cookies are best the day after baking.

Makes 3 dozen cookies

- Sell It -
Stack cookies, brownies and bars high on colorful plastic or heavy paper plates.

Raspberry Pecan Thumbprints

No-Bake Gingersnap Balls

20 gingersnap cookies (about 5 ounces)
3 tablespoons dark corn syrup
2 tablespoons creamy peanut butter
⅓ cup powdered sugar

1 Place cookies in large resealable plastic food storage bag; crush finely with rolling pin or meat mallet.

2 Combine corn syrup and peanut butter in medium bowl. Add crushed gingersnaps; mix well. (Mixture should hold together without being sticky. If mixture is too dry, stir in additional tablespoon corn syrup.)

3 Roll mixture into 24 (1-inch) balls; coat with powdered sugar. Makes 2 dozen cookies

- Sell It -
For buyers who want an assortment of cookies, offer several varieties in small packages of six or eight. To prevent transfer of flavors and changes in texture, do not mix different cookies in the same package.

No-Bake Peanutty Cookies

2 cups Roasted Honey Nut SKIPPY® Creamy or SUPER CHUNK® Peanut Butter
2 cups graham cracker crumbs
1 cup confectioners' sugar
½ cup KARO® Light or Dark Corn Syrup
¼ cup semisweet chocolate chips, melted
Colored sprinkles (optional)

1 In large bowl, combine peanut butter, graham cracker crumbs, confectioners' sugar and corn syrup. Mix until smooth. Shape into 1-inch balls. Place on waxed-paper-lined cookie sheet.

2 Drizzle melted chocolate over balls; roll in colored sprinkles, if desired. Store covered in refrigerator.
Makes about 5 dozen cookies

- Make It Special -
Nothing makes a cookie stand out more than being partially or completely covered in chocolate! Simply dip cookies in melted chocolate (milk, dark, white or some of each) and place on waxed paper until chocolate is set.

No-Bake Gingersnap Balls

Peanut Butter Chocolate Stars

1 cup peanut butter
1 cup packed light brown sugar
1 egg
48 milk chocolate candy stars or other solid milk chocolate candy

Preheat oven to 350°F. Line cookie sheets with parchment paper or leave ungreased. Combine peanut butter, sugar and egg in medium bowl until blended and smooth.

Shape dough into 48 balls about 1½ inches in diameter. Place 2 inches apart on cookie sheets. Press one chocolate star on top of each cookie. Bake 10 to 12 minutes or until set. Transfer to wire racks to cool completely.

Makes 4 dozen cookies

Peanut Butter Crisscross Cookies: *Prepare dough and shape cookies as directed above, omitting chocolate stars. Dip fork into granulated sugar; press crisscross fashion onto each cookie, flattening to ½-inch thickness. Bake as directed above.*

Hershey®s Soft & Chewy Cookies

Hershey's Soft & Chewy Cookies

1 cup (2 sticks) butter (no substitutes)
¾ cup packed light brown sugar
½ cup granulated sugar
¼ cup light corn syrup
1 egg
2 teaspoons vanilla extract
2½ cups all-purpose flour
1 teaspoon baking soda
¼ teaspoon salt
1 package (10 or 12 ounces) HERSHEY'S Chips or Baking Bits (any flavor)

1 Heat oven to 350°F.

2 In large bowl, beat butter and sugars until light and fluffy. Add corn syrup, egg and vanilla; beat well. Stir together flour, baking soda and salt; gradually add to butter mixture, beating until blended. Stir in chips. Drop by rounded teaspoons onto ungreased cookie sheets.

3 Bake 8 to 10 minutes or until lightly browned and almost set. Cool slightly; remove from cookie sheets to wire racks. Cool completely. Cookies will be softer the second day.
Makes about 3½ dozen cookies

Chocolate Chocolate Cookies:
Decrease flour to 2¼ cups and add ¼ cup HERSHEY'S Cocoa or HERSHEY'S European Style Cocoa.

Fresh Orange Cookies

1½ cups all-purpose flour
½ teaspoon baking soda
¼ teaspoon salt
½ cup butter or margarine, softened
½ cup granulated sugar
½ cup packed light brown sugar
1 egg
1 unpeeled SUNKIST® Orange, finely chopped*
½ cup chopped walnuts
Orange Glaze (recipe follows)

*Chop orange in blender, food processor or by hand, to equal ¾ cup.

Sift together flour, baking soda and salt. In large bowl, beat butter and sugars until light and fluffy. Add egg and chopped orange; beat well. Gradually blend in flour mixture. Stir in walnuts. Cover and chill at least 1 hour. Drop dough by teaspoons onto lightly greased cookie sheets. Bake at 375°F for 10 to 12 minutes. Cool on wire racks. Spread cookies with Orange Glaze.
Makes about 4 dozen cookies

Orange Glaze

1 cup confectioners' sugar
1 to 2 tablespoons fresh orange juice
1 tablespoon butter or margarine, softened
1 teaspoon grated orange peel

In small bowl, combine all ingredients until smooth.
Makes about ½ cup

Peanut Butter Bears

1 cup **SKIPPY® Creamy Peanut Butter**
1 cup **(2 sticks) MAZOLA® Margarine or butter, softened**
1 cup **firmly packed brown sugar**
²⁄₃ cup **KARO® Light or Dark Corn Syrup**
2 **eggs**
4 **cups flour, divided**
1 **tablespoon baking powder**
1 **teaspoon ground cinnamon (optional)**
¼ **teaspoon salt**

1 In large bowl with mixer at medium speed, beat peanut butter, margarine, brown sugar, corn syrup and eggs until smooth. Reduce speed; beat in 2 cups flour, baking powder, cinnamon and salt. With spoon, stir in remaining 2 cups flour. Wrap dough in plastic wrap; refrigerate 2 hours.

2 Preheat oven to 325°F. Divide dough in half.

3 On floured surface, roll out half the dough to ⅛-inch thickness. Cut with floured bear cookie cutter. Repeat with remaining dough.

4 Bake on ungreased cookie sheets 10 minutes or until lightly browned. Remove from cookie sheets; cool completely on wire racks. Decorate as desired.

Makes about 3 dozen bears

Prep time: 35 minutes, plus chilling
Bake time: 10 minutes, plus cooling

Note: *Use scraps of dough to make bear faces. Form one small ball of dough for muzzle and 3 smaller balls of dough for eyes and nose. Gently press scraps onto unbaked cookies and bake as directed. If desired, use frosting to create paws, ears and bow ties.*

- Sell It -

Display small packages of cookies and individually wrapped baked goods in large wide baskets lined with colorful napkins or kitchen towels. If your only baskets are tall and narrow, turn them on their sides and display baked goods spilling out of them.

Peanut Butter Bears

Oatmeal Raisin Cookies

¾ **cup all-purpose flour**
¾ **teaspoon salt**
½ **teaspoon baking soda**
½ **teaspoon ground cinnamon**
¾ **cup (1½ sticks) butter or margarine, softened**
¾ **cup granulated sugar**
¾ **cup packed light brown sugar**
1 **egg**
1 **tablespoon water**
1 **tablespoon vanilla, divided**
3 **cups uncooked quick or old-fashioned oats**
1 **cup raisins**
½ **cup powdered sugar**
1 **tablespoon milk**

Preheat oven to 375°F. Grease cookie sheets; set aside. Combine flour, salt, baking soda and cinnamon in small bowl.

Beat butter, granulated sugar and brown sugar in large bowl with electric mixer at medium speed until light and fluffy. Add egg, water and 2 teaspoons vanilla; beat well. Add flour mixture; beat at low speed just until blended. Stir in oats with spoon. Stir in raisins. Drop tablespoonfuls of dough 2 inches apart onto prepared cookie sheets.

Bake 10 to 11 minutes or until edges are golden brown. Let cookies stand 2 minutes on cookie sheets; transfer to wire racks to cool completely.

For glaze, stir powdered sugar, milk and remaining 1 teaspoon vanilla in small bowl until smooth. Drizzle over cookies with fork or spoon. Store cookies tightly covered at room temperature or freeze up to 3 months.

Makes about 4 dozen cookies

- Make It Special -

For a quick decorating trick, drizzle cookies with melted chocolate or a glaze. The contrast of a white drizzle on a chocolate cookie is a sure eye-catcher.

Oatmeal Raisin Cookies

Harvest Pumpkin Cookies

2 cups all-purpose flour
1 teaspoon baking powder
1 teaspoon ground cinnamon
½ teaspoon baking soda
½ teaspoon salt
½ teaspoon ground allspice
1 cup (2 sticks) butter, softened
1 cup sugar
1 cup canned pumpkin
1 large egg
1 teaspoon vanilla
1 cup chopped pecans
1 cup dried cranberries
   (optional)
   Pecan halves (about 36)

1 Preheat oven to 375°F. Place flour, baking powder, cinnamon, baking soda, salt and allspice in medium bowl; stir to combine.

2 Beat butter and sugar in large bowl with electric mixer at medium speed until light and fluffy. Beat in pumpkin, egg and vanilla. Gradually add flour mixture; beat at low speed until well blended. Stir in chopped pecans and cranberries.

3 Drop heaping tablespoonfuls of dough 2 inches apart onto ungreased cookie sheets. Flatten mounds slightly with back of spoon. Press one pecan half into center of each mound. Bake 10 to 12 minutes or until golden brown.

4 Let cookies stand on cookie sheets 1 minute. Remove cookies to wire racks; cool completely. Store tightly covered at room temperature or freeze up to 3 months.

Makes about 3 dozen cookies

Double Almond Butter Cookies

2 cups softened butter
2½ cups powdered sugar, sifted, divided
4 cups flour
2¼ teaspoons vanilla, divided
⅔ cup BLUE DIAMOND® Blanched Almond Paste
¼ cup firmly packed light brown sugar
½ cup BLUE DIAMOND® Chopped Natural Almonds, toasted

Beat butter with 1 cup powdered sugar. Gradually beat in flour. Beat in 2 teaspoons vanilla. Cover and chill dough 30 minutes. Combine almond paste, brown sugar, almonds and remaining ¼ teaspoon vanilla. Shape dough around ½ teaspoon almond paste mixture, completely enclosing almond paste center and forming 1-inch balls. Place on ungreased baking pans. Bake in preheated 350°F oven 15 minutes. Cool. Roll cookies in remaining 1½ cups powdered sugar or sift powdered sugar over cookies.

Makes 8 dozen cookies

Harvest Pumpkin Cookies

Crispy Oat Drops

- 1 **cup (2 sticks) butter or margarine, softened**
- ½ **cup granulated sugar**
- ½ **cup firmly packed light brown sugar**
- 1 **large egg**
- 2 **cups all-purpose flour**
- ½ **cup quick-cooking or old-fashioned oats, uncooked**
- 1 **teaspoon cream of tartar**
- ½ **teaspoon baking soda**
- ¼ **teaspoon salt**
- 1¾ **cups "M & M's"® Semi-Sweet Chocolate Mini Baking Bits**
- 1 **cup toasted rice cereal**
- ½ **cup shredded coconut**
- ½ **cup coarsely chopped pecans**

Preheat oven to 350°F. In large bowl cream butter and sugars until light and fluffy; beat in egg. In medium bowl combine flour, oats, cream of tartar, baking soda and salt; blend flour mixture into butter mixture. Stir in "M & M's"® Semi-Sweet Chocolate Mini Baking Bits, cereal, coconut and pecans. Drop by heaping tablespoonfuls about 2 inches apart onto ungreased cookie sheets. Bake 10 to 13 minutes or until lightly browned. Cool completely on wire racks. Store in tightly covered container.

Makes about 4 dozen cookies

Hershey's Milk Chocolate Chip Giant Cookies

6 tablespoons butter or margarine, softened
½ cup granulated sugar
¼ cup packed light brown sugar
½ teaspoon vanilla extract
1 egg
1 cup all-purpose flour
½ teaspoon baking soda
2 cups (11.5-ounce package) HERSHEY'S Milk Chocolate Chips
Frosting (optional)
Ice cream (optional)

1 Heat oven to 350°F. Line two 9-inch round baking pans with foil, extending foil over edges.

2 Beat butter, granulated sugar, brown sugar and vanilla until light and fluffy. Add egg; beat well. Stir together flour and baking soda; gradually add to butter mixture, beating until well blended. Stir in milk chocolate chips. Spread one half of batter into each prepared pan, spreading to within 1 inch from edge. (Cookies will spread to edge during baking.)

3 Bake 15 to 20 minutes or until lightly browned. Cool completely; carefully lift cookies from pan and remove foil. Frost, if desired. Cut each cookie into 8 wedges; serve topped with scoop of ice cream, if desired.

Makes about 16 servings

Double Chocolate Peanut Cookies made with Snickers® Bars

¾ cup margarine, softened
⅓ cup granulated sugar
⅓ cup firmly packed light brown sugar
1 large egg
1 teaspoon vanilla extract
1½ cups all-purpose flour
2 tablespoons cocoa powder
¾ teaspoon baking soda
¼ teaspoon salt
4 SNICKERS® Bars (2.07 ounces each), coarsely chopped

Preheat oven to 350°F.

In large mixing bowl, cream margarine and sugars. Add egg and vanilla; beat until light and fluffy. Combine flour, cocoa powder, baking soda and salt; gradually blend into creamed mixture. Stir in chopped Snickers® Bars until evenly blended. Drop by heaping tablespoonfuls about 2 inches apart onto ungreased cookie sheets. Bake 9 to 13 minutes. Cool 1 minute on cookie sheets; remove to wire racks. Store in tightly covered container.

Makes about 3 dozen cookies

Hershey's Milk Chocolate Chip Giant Cookies

Outrageous Brownies & Bars

Praline Bars

¾ cup (1½ sticks) butter or
    margarine, softened
1 cup sugar, divided
1 teaspoon vanilla, divided
1½ cups flour
2 packages (8 ounces each)
    PHILADELPHIA
    BRAND® Cream Cheese,
    softened
2 eggs
½ cup almond brickle chips
3 tablespoons caramel ice
    cream topping

MIX butter, ½ cup of the sugar and
½ teaspoon of the vanilla with
electric mixer on medium speed
until light and fluffy. Gradually add
flour, mixing on low speed until
blended. Press onto bottom of
13×9-inch baking pan. Bake at
350°F for 20 to 23 minutes or until
lightly browned.

MIX cream cheese, remaining ½
cup sugar and ½ teaspoon vanilla
with electric mixer on medium
speed until well blended. Add eggs;
mix well. Blend in chips. Pour over
crust. Dot top of cream cheese
mixture with caramel topping. Cut
through batter with knife several
times for marble effect.

BAKE at 350°F for 30 minutes.
Cool in pan on wire rack.
Refrigerate. Cut into bars.
Makes 2 dozen bars

- Sell It -
Include storage directions for any
perishable items that should be
held in the refrigerator.

Praline Bars

26

Outrageous Brownies

Outrageous Brownies

½ cup MIRACLE WHIP® Salad
    Dressing
2 eggs, beaten
¼ cup cold water
1 (21½-ounce) package fudge
    brownie mix
3 (7-ounce) milk chocolate bars,
    divided
    Walnut halves (optional)

PREHEAT oven to 350°F.

MIX together salad dressing, eggs
and water until well blended. Stir in
brownie mix, mixing just until
moistened.

Coarsely **CHOP** two chocolate
bars; stir into brownie mixture.
Pour into greased 13×9-inch
baking pan.

BAKE 30 to 35 minutes or until
edges begin to pull away from sides
of pan. Immediately top with 1
chopped chocolate bar. Let stand
about 5 minutes or until melted;
spread evenly over brownies.
Garnish with walnut halves, if
desired. Cool. Cut into squares.
    Makes about 24 brownies

Prep time: 10 minutes
Bake time: 35 minutes

28

Banana Chocolate Chip Bars

1 cup plus 2 tablespoons all-purpose flour
1 cup plus 2 tablespoons rolled oats
¼ cup plus 2 tablespoons DOLE® Chopped Almonds, toasted
½ teaspoon baking soda
¼ teaspoon salt
¾ cup packed brown sugar
½ cup margarine
2 small, ripe DOLE® Bananas, peeled
½ cup chocolate chips
½ teaspoon grated orange peel

• Combine flour, oats, almonds, baking soda and salt.

• Beat sugar and margarine until light and fluffy. Add flour mixture and beat until well combined. Press half of mixture into 8-inch square baking pan coated with vegetable spray. Bake in 350°F oven 10 to 12 minutes. Cool.

• Dice bananas (1½ cups). Combine with chocolate chips and orange peel. Spread over cooked crust. Top with remaining flour mixture. Press lightly. Bake 20 to 25 minutes until golden.

• Cut into bars.   Makes 12 bars

Prep time: 20 minutes
Bake time: 35 minutes

Almond Toffee Squares

1 cup (2 sticks) margarine or butter, softened
1 cup firmly packed brown sugar
1 egg
1 teaspoon vanilla
2 cups all-purpose flour
¼ teaspoon salt
2 (4-ounce) packages BAKER'S® GERMAN'S® Sweet Chocolate, broken into squares
½ cup toasted slivered almonds
½ cup lightly toasted BAKER'S® ANGEL FLAKE® Coconut

PREHEAT oven to 350°F.

BEAT margarine, sugar, egg and vanilla. Mix in flour and salt. Press into greased 13×9-inch pan.

BAKE for 30 minutes or until edges are golden brown. Remove from oven. Immediately sprinkle with chocolate squares. Cover with foil; let stand 5 minutes or until chocolate is softened.

SPREAD chocolate evenly over entire surface; sprinkle with almonds and coconut. Cut into squares while still warm. Cool on wire rack.

Makes about 26 squares

Prep time: 20 minutes
Bake time: 30 minutes

Reese's® Bits Blondies

⅔ cup butter or margarine, softened
1 cup packed light brown sugar
½ cup granulated sugar
¾ cup REESE'S® Creamy or REESE'S® Crunchy Peanut Butter
2 eggs
1 teaspoon vanilla extract
⅓ cup milk
1¾ cups all-purpose flour
1 teaspoon baking powder
1⅓ cups (10-ounce package) REESE'S® Bits for Baking, divided
Chocolate Brownie Frosting (recipe follows)

1 Heat oven to 325°F. Grease 13×9×2-inch baking pan.

2 In large bowl, beat butter, brown sugar, granulated sugar and peanut butter until creamy. Add eggs and vanilla; beat well. Gradually beat in milk. Gradually beat in flour and baking powder, beating thoroughly. Stir in 1 cup baking bits. Spread batter into prepared pan.

3 Bake 40 to 45 minutes or until wooden pick inserted in center comes out clean. Cool completely in pan on wire rack. Meanwhile, prepare Chocolate Brownie Frosting; spread over top of blondies. Sprinkle remaining ⅓ cup bits on top. Cut into bars.

Makes about 36 bars

Chocolate Brownie Frosting

¼ cup (½ stick) butter or margarine, softened
¼ cup HERSHEY'S Cocoa
1 tablespoon light corn syrup
2 tablespoons milk
1 teaspoon vanilla extract
1½ cups powdered sugar

In medium bowl, beat butter, cocoa, corn syrup, milk and vanilla until smooth. Gradually add powdered sugar, beating until spreading consistency.

Makes about 1¼ cups frosting

- Sell It -
Bake single layer cakes, brownies or bars in foil pans; cover with plastic wrap and tie with a ribbon.

Reese's® Bits Blondies

Rocky Road Brownies

½ cup (1 stick) butter or margarine
½ cup unsweetened cocoa
1 cup sugar
1 egg
½ cup all-purpose flour
¼ cup buttermilk
1 teaspoon vanilla
1 cup miniature marshmallows
1 cup coarsely chopped walnuts
1 cup (6 ounces) semisweet chocolate chips

Preheat oven to 350°F. Lightly grease 8-inch square pan. Combine butter and cocoa in heavy medium saucepan over low heat, stirring constantly until smooth. Remove from heat; stir in sugar, egg, flour, buttermilk and vanilla. Mix until smooth. Spread batter evenly in prepared pan. Bake 25 minutes or until center feels dry. *Do not overbake or brownies will be dry.* Remove from oven; sprinkle marshmallows, walnuts and chocolate chips over top. Return to oven for 3 to 5 minutes or just until topping is warm enough to hold together. Cool in pan on wire rack. Cut into 2-inch squares.

Makes 16 brownies

Moist and Minty Brownies

1¼ cups all-purpose flour
½ teaspoon baking soda
¼ teaspoon salt
¾ cup granulated sugar
½ cup (1 stick) butter or margarine
2 tablespoons water
1½ cups (10-ounce package) NESTLÉ® Toll House® Mint-Chocolate Morsels, divided
1 teaspoon vanilla extract
2 eggs

COMBINE flour, baking soda and salt in small bowl. Combine sugar, butter and water in medium saucepan. Bring *just to a boil* over medium heat, stirring constantly; remove from heat.* Add *1 cup* morsels and vanilla; stir until smooth. Add eggs, one at a time, stirring well after each addition. Stir in flour mixture and *remaining* morsels. Spread into greased 9-inch square baking pan.

BAKE in preheated 350°F. oven for 20 to 30 minutes or until center is set. Cool in pan on wire rack (center will sink).

Makes 16 brownies

Or, combine sugar, butter and water in medium microwave-safe bowl. Microwave on HIGH (100%) power for 3 minutes, stirring halfway through cooking time. Stir until smooth. Proceed as above.

Heavenly Oat Bars

½ cup (1 stick) MAZOLA®
   Margarine, softened
½ cup packed brown sugar
½ cup KARO® Light or Dark
   Corn Syrup
1 teaspoon vanilla
3 cups uncooked quick or
   old-fashioned oats
1 cup (6 ounces) semisweet
   chocolate chips
½ cup SKIPPY® Creamy Peanut
   Butter

1 Preheat oven to 350°F. Lightly grease 9-inch square baking pan.

2 In large bowl with mixer at medium speed, beat margarine, brown sugar, corn syrup and vanilla until blended and smooth. Stir in oats. Spread in prepared pan.

3 Bake 25 minutes or until center is just firm. Cool slightly.

4 In small heavy saucepan over low heat, stir chocolate chips until melted and smooth. Remove from heat; stir in peanut butter until smooth. Spread over warm bars. Cool completely on wire rack before cutting.   Makes 24 bars

Prep time: 15 minutes
Bake time: 25 minutes, plus cooling

Tip: *To melt chocolate chips in microwave, place chips in dry microwavable bowl. Microwave on HIGH (100%) 1 minute; stir. Microwave 1 minute longer. Stir until smooth.*

Raspberry Coconut Layer Bars

1⅔ cups graham cracker crumbs
½ cup (1 stick) butter or
   margarine, melted
2⅔ cups (7-ounce package) flaked
   coconut
1¼ cups (14-ounce can)
   CARNATION® Sweetened
   Condensed Milk
1 cup raspberry jam or
   preserves
⅓ cup finely chopped walnuts,
   toasted
½ cup NESTLÉ® Toll House®
   Semi-Sweet Chocolate
   Morsels, melted
¼ cup (1½ ounces) NESTLÉ®
   Premier White Baking Bar,
   melted

COMBINE graham cracker crumbs and butter in medium bowl. Spread evenly on bottom of 13×9-inch baking pan; press in firmly. Sprinkle with coconut; pour sweetened condensed milk evenly over coconut.

BAKE in preheated 350°F. oven for 20 to 25 minutes or until lightly browned; cool for 15 minutes.

SPREAD jam over coconut layer; chill for 3 to 4 hours or until firm. Sprinkle with nuts. Drizzle with melted morsels and baking bar; chill. Cut into 3×1½-inch bars.
   Makes 24 bar cookies

One Bowl™ Brownies

4 squares BAKER'S®
    Unsweetened Chocolate
¾ cup (1½ sticks) margarine or
    butter
2 cups sugar
3 eggs
1 teaspoon vanilla
1 cup all-purpose flour
1 cup chopped nuts (optional)

PREHEAT oven to 350°F.

MICROWAVE chocolate and margarine in large microwavable bowl on HIGH 2 minutes or until margarine is melted. **Stir until chocolate is completely melted.**

STIR sugar into melted chocolate mixture. Mix in eggs and vanilla until well blended. Stir in flour and nuts. Spread evenly in greased 13×9-inch pan.

BAKE for 30 to 35 minutes or until wooden pick inserted in center comes out with fudgy crumbs. **Do not overbake.** Cool in pan; cut into squares.

         Makes about 24 brownies

Prep time: 10 minutes
Bake time: 30 to 35 minutes

Peanut Butter Swirl Brownies:
Prepare One Bowl™ Brownies as directed, reserving 1 tablespoon of the margarine and 2 tablespoons of the sugar. Add reserved ingredients to ⅔ cup peanut butter; mix well.

Place spoonfuls of peanut butter mixture over brownie batter. Swirl with knife to marbleize. Bake for 30 to 35 minutes or until wooden pick inserted into center comes out with fudgy crumbs. Cool in pan; cut into squares. Makes about 24 brownies.

Prep time: 15 minutes
Bake time: 30 to 35 minutes

Rocky Road Brownies: *Prepare One Bowl™ Brownies as directed. Bake for 30 minutes. Sprinkle 2 cups miniature marshmallows, 1 cup BAKER'S® Semi-Sweet Real Chocolate Chips and 1 cup chopped nuts over brownies immediately. Continue baking 3 to 5 minutes or until topping begins to melt together. Cool in pan; cut into squares. Makes about 24 brownies.*

Prep time: 15 minutes
Bake time: 35 minutes

- Make It Special -

For easy removal of brownies and bar cookies (and no cleanup!), line the baking pan with foil and leave at least 3 inches hanging over on each side. Lift the brownies or bars out of the pan using the foil and place them on a cutting board. Remove the foil and cut the treats into pieces.

Rainbow Blondies

- **1 cup (2 sticks) butter or margarine, softened**
- **1½ cups firmly packed light brown sugar**
- **1 large egg**
- **1 teaspoon vanilla extract**
- **2 cups all-purpose flour**
- **½ teaspoon baking soda**
- **1¾ cups "M & M's"® Semi-Sweet or Milk Chocolate Mini Baking Bits**
- **1 cup chopped walnuts or pecans**

Preheat oven to 350°F. Lightly grease 13×9×2-inch baking pan; set aside. In large bowl cream butter and sugar until light and fluffy; beat in egg and vanilla. In medium bowl combine flour and baking soda; add to creamed mixture just until combined. *Dough will be stiff.* Stir in "M & M's"® Semi-Sweet Chocolate Mini Baking Bits and nuts. Spread dough into prepared baking pan. Bake 30 to 35 minutes or until toothpick inserted in center comes out with moist crumbs. *Do not overbake.* Cool completely. Cut into bars. Store in tightly covered container.

Makes 24 bars

One Bowl™ Brownies

Peachy Oatmeal Bars

Peachy Oatmeal Bars

CRUMB MIXTURE
- 1½ cups all-purpose flour
- 1 cup quick oats
- ½ cup sugar
- ¾ cup (1½ sticks) margarine, melted
- ½ teaspoon baking soda
- ¼ teaspoon salt
- 2 teaspoons almond extract

FILLING
- ¾ cup peach preserves
- ⅓ cup flaked coconut

Preheat oven to 350°F. For crumb mixture, in large bowl, combine all crumb mixture ingredients. Beat at low speed, scraping bowl often, until mixture is crumbly, 1 to 2 minutes. Reserve ¾ cup crumb mixture; press remaining crumb mixture onto bottom of greased 9-inch square baking pan.

For filling, spread peach preserves to within ½ inch of edges of crumb mixture; sprinkle reserved crumb mixture and coconut over top. Bake 22 to 27 minutes or until edges are lightly browned. Cool completely. Cut into bars.

Makes 24 to 30 bars

Extra Moist & Chunky Brownies

- 1 (8-ounce) package cream cheese, softened
- 1 cup sugar
- 1 egg
- 1 teaspoon vanilla extract
- ¾ cup all-purpose flour
- 1 (4-serving size) package ROYAL® Chocolate or Dark 'N' Sweet Chocolate Pudding & Pie Filling
- 4 (1-ounce) semisweet chocolate squares, chopped

In large bowl with electric mixer at high speed, beat cream cheese, sugar, egg and vanilla until smooth; blend in flour and pudding mix. Spread batter in greased 8×8-inch microwavable dish; sprinkle with chopped chocolate. Microwave at HIGH (100% power) for 8 to 10 minutes or until toothpick inserted in center comes out clean, rotating dish ½ turn every 2 minutes. Cool completely in pan. Cut into squares.

Makes about 16 brownies

- Sell It -
Dress up a sale table with bright fabric, inexpensive tablecloths or pots of colorful flowers.

Apple Crumb Squares

- 2 cups QUAKER® Oats (Quick or Old Fashioned), uncooked
- 1½ cups all-purpose flour
- 1 cup packed brown sugar
- ¾ cup butter or margarine, melted
- 1 teaspoon ground cinnamon
- ½ teaspoon baking soda
- ½ teaspoon salt (optional)
- ¼ teaspoon ground nutmeg
- 1 cup applesauce
- ½ cup chopped nuts

Preheat oven to 350°F. In large bowl, combine all ingredients except applesauce and nuts; mix until crumbly. Reserve 1 cup oats mixture. Press remaining mixture onto bottom of greased 13×9-inch pan. Bake 13 to 15 minutes; cool. Spread applesauce over partially baked crust; sprinkle with nuts. Sprinkle reserved 1 cup oats mixture over top. Bake 13 to 15 minutes or until golden brown. Cool in pan on wire rack; cut into 2-inch squares.

Makes about 24 squares

Caramel-Layered Brownies

4 squares BAKER'S®
   Unsweetened Chocolate
¾ cup (1½ sticks) margarine or
   butter
2 cups sugar
3 eggs
1 teaspoon vanilla
1 cup all-purpose flour
1 cup BAKER'S® Semi-Sweet
   Real Chocolate Chips
1½ cups chopped nuts
1 package (14 ounces) caramels
⅓ cup evaporated milk

HEAT oven to 350°F.

MICROWAVE chocolate and margarine in large microwavable bowl on HIGH 2 minutes or until margarine is melted. **Stir until chocolate is completely melted.**

STIR sugar into melted chocolate mixture. Mix in eggs and vanilla until well blended. Stir in flour. Remove 1 cup of batter; set aside. Spread remaining batter in greased 13×9-inch pan. Sprinkle with chips and 1 cup nuts.

MICROWAVE caramels and milk in same bowl on HIGH 4 minutes, stirring after 2 minutes. Stir until caramels are completely melted and smooth. Spoon over chips and nuts, spreading to edges of pan. Gently spread reserved batter over caramel mixture. Sprinkle with remaining ½ cup nuts.

BAKE for 40 minutes or until toothpick inserted into center comes out with fudgy crumbs. **Do not overbake.** Cool in pan; cut into squares.

Makes about 24 brownies

Prep time: 20 minutes
Bake time: 40 minutes

No-Fuss Bar Cookies

2 cups graham cracker crumbs
   (about 24 graham cracker
   squares)
1 cup semisweet chocolate chips
1 cup flaked coconut
¾ cup coarsely chopped walnuts
1 can (14 ounces) sweetened
   condensed milk

Preheat oven to 350°F. Combine crumbs, chips, coconut and walnuts in medium bowl; toss to blend. Add milk; mix until blended. Spread batter into greased 13×9-inch baking pan. Bake 15 to 18 minutes or until edges are golden brown. Let pan stand on wire rack until completely cooled. Cut into 2¼-inch squares.

Makes about 20 bars

No-Fuss Bar Cookies

Spectacular Cakes

Mini Morsel Pound Cake

3 cups all-purpose flour
1 teaspoon baking powder
½ teaspoon salt
2 cups granulated sugar
1 cup (2 sticks) butter or
  margarine, softened
1 tablespoon vanilla extract
4 eggs
¾ cup milk
2 cups (12-ounce package)
  NESTLÉ® TOLL HOUSE®
  Semi-Sweet Chocolate Mini
  Morsels
  Powdered sugar

COMBINE flour, baking powder and salt in small bowl. Beat sugar, butter and vanilla in large mixing bowl until well blended. Beat in eggs one at a time, beating well after each addition. Gradually beat in flour mixture alternately with milk. Stir in morsels. Pour into greased and floured 10-inch Bundt pan or two greased and floured 9×5-inch loaf pans.

BAKE in preheated 325°F. oven for 1 hour 5 minutes to 1 hour 15 minutes or until wooden pick inserted near center comes out clean. Cool in pan on wire rack for 15 minutes. Remove from pan; serve warm or cool completely on wire rack. Sprinkle with powdered sugar before serving.

Makes 16 servings

Mini Morsel Pound Cake

Chocolate Cheesecake Cupcakes

CUPCAKES

- 2 cups (12-ounce package) NESTLÉ® TOLL HOUSE® Semi-Sweet Chocolate Morsels, divided
- 1½ cups all-purpose flour
- 1 teaspoon baking soda
- ½ teaspoon salt
- ½ cup granulated sugar
- ⅓ cup vegetable oil
- 1 egg
- 1 teaspoon vanilla extract
- 1 cup water

FILLING

- 2 packages (3 ounces each) cream cheese, softened
- ¼ cup granulated sugar
- 1 egg
- ⅛ teaspoon salt

FOR CUPCAKES:

MICROWAVE *½ cup* morsels in small, microwave-safe bowl on HIGH (100%) power for 45 seconds; stir. Microwave at additional 10- to 20-second intervals, stirring until smooth; cool to room temperature.

COMBINE flour, baking soda and salt in small bowl. Beat sugar, oil, egg and vanilla in large mixer bowl until blended. Beat in melted chocolate; gradually beat in flour mixture alternately with water (batter will be thin).

FOR FILLING:

BEAT cream cheese, sugar, egg and salt in small mixer bowl until creamy. Stir in *1 cup* morsels.

TO ASSEMBLE:

SPOON cupcake batter into 16 greased or paper-lined muffin cups, filling ½ full. Spoon filling by rounded tablespoons over batter. Spoon remaining batter over filling. Bake in preheated 350°F. oven for 20 to 25 minutes or until wooden pick inserted in center comes out clean. While still hot, sprinkle with *remaining ½ cup* morsels. Let stand for 5 minutes or until morsels are shiny; spread to frost. Remove to wire racks to cool completely.

Makes 16 cupcakes

- Sell It -

For school bake sales, have students decorate clean, sturdy gift boxes and line them with brightly colored tissue paper for packing cupcakes, cookies, brownies, bars and muffins.

Chocolate Cheesecake Cupcakes

Deep Dark Chocolate Cake

2 cups sugar
1¾ cups all-purpose flour
¾ cup HERSHEY'S Cocoa or HERSHEY'S European Style Cocoa
1½ teaspoons baking powder
1½ teaspoons baking soda
1 teaspoon salt
2 eggs
1 cup milk
½ cup vegetable oil
2 teaspoons vanilla extract
1 cup boiling water
One-Bowl Buttercream Frosting (recipe follows)

Heat oven to 350°F. Grease and flour two 9-inch round baking pans.* In large bowl, stir together sugar, flour, cocoa, baking powder, baking soda and salt. Add eggs, milk, oil and vanilla; beat on medium speed of mixer 2 minutes. Stir in water. (Batter will be thin.) Pour batter into prepared pans. Bake 30 to 35 minutes or until wooden pick inserted in center comes out clean. Cool 10 minutes; remove from pans to wire racks. Cool completely. Prepare One-Bowl Buttercream Frosting; frost cake.

Makes 8 to 10 servings

*One 13×9×2-inch baking pan may be substituted for two 9-inch round baking pans. Prepare as directed above. Bake 35 to 40 minutes. Cool completely in pan. Frost as desired.

One-Bowl Buttercream Frosting

6 tablespoons butter or margarine, softened
2⅔ cups powdered sugar
½ cup HERSHEY'S Cocoa or HERSHEY'S European Style Cocoa
⅓ cup milk
1 teaspoon vanilla extract

In medium bowl, beat butter. Blend in powdered sugar and cocoa alternately with milk, beating well after each addition until smooth and of spreading consistency. Blend in vanilla. Add additional milk, if needed.

- Make It Special -

Try this easy trick to make chocolate curls: Allow a square of semisweet or bittersweet chocolate to soften slightly in a warm place for 30 minutes; then make curls by drawing a vegetable peeler across the bottom of the square. Transfer curls to a waxed-paper-lined tray with a wooden toothpick and chill until firm.

Coconut Cupcakes

1 package DUNCAN HINES®
    Moist Deluxe Butter Recipe
    Golden Cake Mix
3 eggs
1 cup (8 ounces) dairy sour
    cream
⅔ cup cream of coconut
¼ cup butter or margarine,
    softened
2 containers (16 ounces each)
    DUNCAN HINES® Creamy
    Homestyle Cream Cheese
    Frosting
2½ cups toasted coconut (see Tip)

1 Preheat oven to 375°F. Place 36 (2½-inch) paper liners in muffin cups.

2 Combine cake mix, eggs, sour cream, cream of coconut and butter in large bowl. Beat at low speed until blended. Beat at medium speed 4 minutes. Fill paper liners half full. Bake 17 to 19 minutes or until toothpick inserted in center comes out clean. Cool in pans 5 minutes. Remove to cooling racks. Cool completely.

3 Frost cupcakes; sprinkle with toasted coconut.

                 Makes 36 cupcakes

Tip: To toast coconut, spread evenly on baking sheet. Toast in preheated 350°F oven for 3 minutes. Stir and toast 1 to 2 minutes longer or until light golden brown.

Chocolate Marble Cheesecake

1 (9-ounce) package
    NABISCO® Famous
    Chocolate Wafers, finely
    rolled
6 tablespoons
    FLEISCHMANN'S®
    Margarine, melted
3 (8-ounce) packages cream
    cheese, softened
1 cup sugar
1½ teaspoons vanilla extract
5 eggs
2 ounces semisweet chocolate,
    melted
2 teaspoons grated orange peel

Mix crumbs and margarine; set aside ½ cup mixture. Press remaining crumbs onto bottom and 1½ inches up side of 9-inch springform pan. Chill.

With mixer, beat cream cheese, sugar and vanilla until light. Beat in eggs, one at a time. Remove 1 cup batter and blend with chocolate and reserved crumb mixture; set aside. Stir orange peel into remaining batter. Pour orange batter into prepared crust; top with spoonfuls of chocolate batter. Using knife, swirl batters to marble. Bake at 300°F for 50 to 60 minutes or until set. Chill 4 hours or overnight.

                 Makes 12 servings

Raspberry-Swirled Cheesecake

14 chocolate sandwich cream cookies
3 tablespoons butter or margarine, melted
1 package (8 ounces) cream cheese, softened
1 cup powdered sugar
1 tablespoon lemon juice
1 teaspoon vanilla
2½ cups thawed nondairy whipped topping
¼ cup seedless raspberry jam
Mint leaves (optional)

Place cookies in food processor or blender; process with on/off pulses until finely crushed. Add butter; process with pulses until blended. Press crumb mixture onto bottom of 8-inch square or round baking dish; refrigerate.

Beat cream cheese in large bowl with electric mixer at medium speed until creamy. Add sugar; beat well. Add lemon juice and vanilla; beat until smooth. Stir in whipped topping. Pour into prepared crust.

Make 20 to 25 holes in cheesecake with teaspoon. Stir jam until smooth. Place jam in holes. Gently swirl jam with tip of knife. Refrigerate cheesecake 2 hours. Garnish with mint leaves, if desired.   Makes 9 servings

Mississippi Nilla® Mud Cake

1½ cups margarine
4 eggs
1 cup unsweetened cocoa
1½ cups all-purpose flour
2 cups granulated sugar
¼ teaspoon salt
1¼ cups PLANTER'S® pecans, chopped
3 cups miniature marshmallows
35 NILLA® Wafers
1 (1-pound) box powdered sugar
½ cup milk
½ teaspoon vanilla extract

Preheat oven to 350°F. In large bowl, with electric mixer at medium speed, beat 1 cup margarine, eggs and ½ cup cocoa until well combined. Blend in flour, granulated sugar, salt and pecans. Spread batter in greased 13×9×2-inch baking pan. Bake at 350°F for 30 to 35 minutes or until cake pulls away from sides of pan. Sprinkle marshmallows over hot cake; return to oven for 2 minutes or until marshmallows are slightly puffed. Arrange wafers over marshmallow layer.

In medium bowl, with mixer at medium speed, beat remaining ½ cup margarine, powdered sugar, remaining ½ cup cocoa, milk and vanilla until smooth; spread immediately over wafers. Cool cake completely on wire rack.
          Makes 24 servings

Raspberry-Swirled Cheesecake

Banana Cake

2½ cups all-purpose flour
1 teaspoon salt
¾ teaspoon baking powder
¾ teaspoon baking soda
1⅔ cups sugar
⅔ cup shortening
2 eggs
1¼ cups mashed ripe bananas
(2 to 3 medium)
⅔ cup buttermilk, divided
⅔ cup chopped walnuts
Frosting (recipe follows)
Banana slices and fresh mint
leaves (optional)

1 Preheat oven to 375°F. Grease and flour two 9-inch round cake pans.

2 Combine flour, salt, baking powder and baking soda in medium bowl; set aside. Beat together sugar and shortening in large bowl with electric mixer until light and fluffy. Add eggs, one at a time, beating well after each addition. Blend in bananas.

3 Add flour mixture alternately with buttermilk, beating well after each addition. Stir in walnuts. Pour evenly into prepared pans.

4 Bake 30 to 35 minutes or until toothpick inserted in center comes out clean. Cool in pans on wire racks 10 minutes. Loosen edges; invert layers onto racks to cool completely.

5 Prepare Frosting. Fill and frost cake layers with Frosting. Run cake comb across top and around side of cake for ridged effect, if desired. Garnish with banana slices and mint, if desired.

Makes 12 servings

Frosting

⅓ cup plus 2 tablespoons
all-purpose flour
Dash salt
1 cup milk
½ cup shortening
½ cup (1 stick) margarine,
softened
1¼ cups granulated sugar
1 teaspoon vanilla

Combine flour and salt in medium saucepan. Gradually stir in milk until well blended. Cook over medium heat until thickened, stirring constantly; cool. Beat together shortening and margarine in large bowl until creamy. Add sugar; beat until light and fluffy. Blend in vanilla. Add flour mixture; beat until smooth.

- Make It Special -

To give a professional look to frosted layer cakes, purchase an inexpensive cake comb. Also known as an icing comb, this flat triangular metal or plastic tool has sawtooth edges to make grooved patterns in frosting.

Banana Cake

New York Cheesecake

1 cup graham cracker crumbs
3 tablespoons sugar
3 tablespoons butter or
    margarine, melted
5 packages (8 ounces each)
    PHILADELPHIA
    BRAND® Cream Cheese,
    softened
1 cup sugar
3 tablespoons flour
1 tablespoon vanilla
3 eggs
1 cup BREAKSTONE'S® or
    KNUDSEN® Sour Cream

1 **MIX** crumbs, 3 tablespoons sugar and butter; press onto bottom of 9-inch springform pan. Bake at 350°F for 10 minutes.

2 **MIX** cream cheese, 1 cup sugar, flour and vanilla with electric mixer on medium speed until well blended. Add eggs, 1 at a time, mixing on low speed after each addition, just until blended. Blend in sour cream. Pour over crust.

3 **BAKE** 1 hour and 5 minutes to 1 hour and 10 minutes or until center is almost set. Run knife or metal spatula around rim of pan to loosen cake; cool before removing rim of pan. Refrigerate 4 hours or overnight. Top with cherry pie filling and garnish, if desired.

Makes 12 servings

Prep time: 15 minutes plus refrigerating
Bake time: 1 hour 10 minutes

Chocolate New York Cheesecake: *Substitute 1 cup chocolate wafer cookie crumbs for graham cracker crumbs. Blend 8 squares BAKER'S® Semi-Sweet Chocolate, melted and slightly cooled, into batter. Continue as directed.*

Lemon Poppy Seed Cupcakes

CUPCAKES
1 package DUNCAN HINES®
    Moist Deluxe Lemon
    Supreme Cake Mix
3 eggs
1⅓ cups water
⅓ cup CRISCO® Oil or
    CRISCO® PURITAN®
    Canola Oil
3 tablespoons poppy seed

LEMON FROSTING
1 container (16 ounces)
    DUNCAN HINES® Creamy
    Homestyle Vanilla Frosting
1 teaspoon grated lemon peel
¼ teaspoon lemon extract
3 to 4 drops yellow food
    coloring
    Gumdrops and other candy,
    for garnish

New York Cheesecake

1 Preheat oven to 350°F. Place 30 (2½-inch) paper liners in muffin cups.

2 **For cupcakes,** combine cake mix, eggs, water, oil and poppy seed in large bowl. Beat at medium speed of electric mixer 2 minutes. Fill paper liners about half full. Bake 18 to 21 minutes or until toothpick inserted in center comes out clean. Cool in pans 5 minutes. Remove to cooling racks. Cool completely.

3 **For Lemon Frosting,** combine Vanilla frosting, lemon peel and lemon extract in small bowl. Tint with yellow food coloring to desired color. Frost cupcakes with Lemon Frosting. Garnish as desired.   Makes 30 cupcakes

Almond Coconut Butter Cake

¾ cup cake flour
1 teaspoon baking powder
¼ teaspoon salt
⅔ cup BLUE DIAMOND® Blanched Almond Paste
¾ cup granulated sugar
2 eggs
1 teaspoon vanilla
½ cup milk
¼ cup plus 2 tablespoons butter, divided
¾ cup brown sugar
1 cup flaked sweetened coconut
¼ cup heavy cream

Sift cake flour, baking powder and salt; reserve. Beat almond paste and granulated sugar with electric mixer until mixture resembles coarse cornmeal. Gradually beat in eggs and vanilla on medium speed, scraping sides of bowl occasionally. Stir in flour mixture. Bring milk and 2 tablespoons butter to a boil; stir into cake batter. Pour into greased 8-inch square pan. Bake at 350°F for 30 minutes or until toothpick inserted in center comes out clean. Meanwhile, combine brown sugar, remaining ¼ cup butter, melted, coconut and cream. Spread over warm cake; place about 5 inches from broiler heat source. Broil about 3 minutes or until top is golden brown.

Makes 9 servings

Polka Dot Pumpkin Cupcakes

TOPPING
½ cup (4 ounces) cream cheese, softened
1 egg
2 tablespoons sugar
⅔ cup NESTLÉ® TOLL HOUSE® Semi-Sweet Chocolate Mini Morsels

CUPCAKES
1 package (16 ounces) pound cake mix
1 cup LIBBY'S® Solid Pack Pumpkin
⅓ cup water
2 eggs
2 teaspoons pumpkin pie spice
1 teaspoon baking soda

FOR TOPPING:

BEAT cream cheese, egg and sugar in small mixing bowl until smooth. Stir in morsels.

FOR CUPCAKES:

COMBINE all cupcake ingredients in large mixing bowl; beat on medium speed for 3 minutes. Pour into 18 paper-lined muffin cups, filling ¾ full. Spoon about 1 tablespoon topping over batter in each cup.

BAKE in preheated 325°F. oven for 25 to 30 minutes or until toothpick inserted in center comes out clean. Cool in pans for 10 minutes. Remove to wire racks to cool.

Makes 18 cupcakes

Mom's Favorite White Cake

2¼ cups cake flour
1 tablespoon baking powder
½ teaspoon salt
½ cup butter or margarine, softened
1½ cups sugar
4 egg whites
2 teaspoons vanilla
1 cup milk
Strawberry Frosting (recipe follows)
Fruit Filling (recipe follows)
Fresh strawberries (optional)

Preheat oven to 350°F. Line bottom of two 9-inch round cake pans with waxed paper; lightly grease paper. Combine flour, baking powder and salt in medium bowl; set aside.

Beat butter and sugar in large bowl with electric mixer at medium speed until light and fluffy. Add egg whites, two at a time, beating well after each addition. Add vanilla; beat until blended. With electric mixer at low speed, add flour mixture alternately with milk, beating well after each addition. Pour batter evenly into prepared pans.

Bake 25 minutes or until toothpick inserted in center comes out clean. Cool layers in pans on wire racks 10 minutes. Loosen edges and invert layers onto racks to cool completely.

Prepare Strawberry Frosting and Fruit Filling. To fill and frost cake, place one layer on cake plate; spread top with Fruit Filling. Place second layer over filling. Frost top and sides with Strawberry Frosting. Place strawberries on top of cake, if desired. Refrigerate; allow cake to stand at room temperature 15 minutes before serving.

Makes 12 servings

Strawberry Frosting

2 envelopes (1.3 ounces each) whipped topping mix
⅔ cup milk
1 cup (6 ounces) white chocolate chips, melted
¼ cup strawberry jam

Beat whipped topping mix and milk in medium bowl with electric mixer at low speed until blended. Beat at high speed 4 minutes until topping thickens and peaks form. With mixer at low speed, beat melted chocolate into topping. Add jam; beat until blended. Chill 15 minutes or until of spreading consistency.

Fruit Filling

1 cup Strawberry Frosting (recipe above)
1 can (8 ounces) crushed pineapple, drained
1 cup sliced strawberries

Combine Strawberry Frosting, pineapple and strawberries in medium bowl; mix well.

Apple Upside-Down Cake

¼ cup (½ stick) plus 3 tablespoons butter or margarine, divided
½ cup packed brown sugar
½ teaspoon ground cinnamon
¼ teaspoon ground nutmeg
¼ teaspoon ground mace
3 apples, peeled, cored and cut into rings
1 tablespoon lemon juice
1⅓ cups all-purpose flour
¾ cup granulated sugar
1½ teaspoons baking powder
¼ teaspoon salt
½ cup milk
1 teaspoon vanilla
1 egg, separated

1 Preheat oven to 375°F. Melt ¼ cup butter in 8-inch square baking pan. Add brown sugar and spices; mix well.

2 Arrange apples over brown sugar mixture on bottom of pan; sprinkle with lemon juice. Set aside.

3 Combine flour, granulated sugar, baking powder and salt in large bowl. Cut in remaining 3 tablespoons butter with pastry blender or 2 knives until mixture resembles coarse crumbs.

4 Add milk and vanilla; beat at low speed with electric mixer until dry ingredients are moistened. Continue beating 2 minutes at medium speed. Blend in egg yolk.

5 Beat egg white in small bowl at high speed with electric mixer until stiff peaks form; gently fold into batter. Pour over apples in pan.

6 Bake 35 minutes or until toothpick inserted in center comes out clean. Cool in pan on wire rack 5 minutes. Loosen edges and invert onto serving plate. Let stand 1 minute before removing pan. Serve warm.

Makes 9 servings

- Make It Special -

When dusting unfrosted cakes or brownies with powdered sugar, add a decorative touch with a paper doily. Just place the doily of your choice on the top of the cake and sprinkle generously with sifted powdered sugar; then carefully remove the doily. Dusting should be done at the last minute. Purchased or homemade stencils can also be used.

Apple Upside-Down Cake

Tantalizing Pies

Fresh Lemon Meringue Pie

1½ cups sugar
¼ cup plus 2 tablespoons cornstarch
½ teaspoon salt
½ cup cold water
½ cup fresh squeezed lemon juice
3 egg yolks, well beaten
2 tablespoons butter or margarine
1½ cups boiling water
Grated peel of ½ SUNKIST® Lemon
2 to 3 drops yellow food coloring (optional)
1 (9-inch) baked pie crust
Three-Egg Meringue (recipe follows)

In large saucepan, combine sugar, cornstarch and salt. Gradually blend in cold water and lemon juice. Stir in egg yolks. Add butter and boiling water. Bring to a boil over medium-high heat, stirring constantly. Reduce heat to medium and boil 1 minute. Remove from heat; stir in lemon peel and food coloring. Pour into baked pie crust. Top with Three-Egg Meringue, sealing well at edges. Bake at 350°F 12 to 15 minutes until meringue is golden brown. Cool 2 hours before serving.

Makes 6 servings

Three-Egg Meringue

3 egg whites
¼ teaspoon cream of tartar
6 tablespoons sugar

In large bowl with electric mixer, beat egg whites with cream of tartar until foamy. Gradually add sugar and beat until stiff peaks form.

Fresh Lemon Merigue Pie

New York Apple Maple Cream Pie

CRUST
9-inch Classic CRISCO®
Double Crust (page 61)

FILLING
6 **cups sliced peeled baking**
apples (about 2 pounds)
1 **cup sugar**
3 **tablespoons cornstarch**
½ **teaspoon salt**
¾ **cup pure maple syrup***
½ **cup whipping cream**

GLAZE
Milk
Sugar

Use maple flavor pancake and waffle syrup, if desired.

1 **For crust,** prepare 9-inch Classic Crisco® Double Crust. Roll and press bottom crust into 9-inch pie plate. Reserve pastry scraps. *Do not bake.* Heat oven to 400°F.

2 **For filling,** place apples, 1 cup sugar, cornstarch and salt in large bowl. Toss to coat. Combine maple syrup and whipping cream in small bowl. Pour over apple mixture. Mix gently. Spoon into unbaked pie crust. Moisten pastry edge with water.

3 Roll top crust. Lift onto filled pie. Trim ½ inch beyond edge of pie plate. Fold top edge under bottom crust. Flute. Decorate with pastry cutouts, if desired. Cut slits in top crust.

4 **For glaze,** brush with milk. Sprinkle with sugar.

5 Bake at 400°F for 50 to 60 minutes or until filling in center is bubbly and crust is golden brown. Refrigerate leftover pie.
Makes 1 (9-inch) pie

Traditional Cherry Pie

3 **cups frozen tart cherries, not**
thawed
1 **cup granulated sugar**
2 **tablespoons quick-cooking**
tapioca
½ **teaspoon almond extract**
Pastry for 2-crust (double)
9-inch pie
2 **tablespoons butter or**
margarine

Preheat oven to 400°F. Combine cherries, sugar, tapioca and almond extract in medium bowl; mix well. Let cherry mixture stand 15 minutes.

Line 9-inch pie plate with 1 pastry crust; fill with cherry mixture. Dot with butter. Cover with top pastry crust. Cut slits in crust for steam to escape. Seal edges and flute.

Bake 50 to 55 minutes or until crust is golden brown and filling is bubbly.   Makes 6 to 8 servings

*Favorite recipe from **Cherry Marketing Institute, Inc.***

New York Apple Maple Cream Pie

Peanut Chocolate Surprise Pie

Peanut Chocolate Surprise Pie

1 cup granulated sugar
8 tablespoons (1 stick) butter, melted
2 eggs
½ cup all-purpose flour
½ cup chopped peanuts
½ cup chopped walnuts
½ cup semisweet chocolate chips
¼ cup bourbon
1 teaspoon vanilla extract
1 (9-inch) unbaked deep-dish pie shell
Whipped cream, for garnish
Chocolate shavings, for garnish

Preheat oven to 350°F. Beat sugar and butter in large bowl until creamy. Add eggs and beat until well mixed. Gradually add flour, then stir in nuts, chips, bourbon and vanilla. Spread mixture evenly in unbaked pie shell. Bake 40 minutes. Cool pie on wire rack; garnish with whipped cream and chocolate shavings.

Makes one 9-inch pie

Oreo® Pecan Fudge Pie

1 (9-inch) OREO® Pie Crust
1 egg white, slightly beaten
1 cup firmly packed light brown sugar
¼ cup FLEISCHMANN'S® Margarine, melted
¾ cup all-purpose flour
1 teaspoon DAVIS® Baking Powder
1 egg
1 teaspoon vanilla extract
1 cup PLANTERS® Gold Measure Pecan Pieces
¼ cup heavy cream
3 (1-ounce) squares semisweet chocolate
Whipped cream, for garnish

Brush pie crust lightly with egg white. Bake at 375°F for 5 minutes; set aside to cool. *Reduce oven temperature to 350°F.*

In medium bowl, with electric mixer at low speed, beat brown sugar and margarine until blended. Blend in flour, baking powder, egg and vanilla; stir in pecans. Spread in prepared crust. Bake at 350°F for 30 to 35 minutes until lightly browned and set. Cool completely.

In saucepan, over low heat, heat heavy cream and chocolate until chocolate melts and mixture is smooth. Remove from heat; cool until thickened. Spread chocolate mixture over cooled pie; chill until set. Garnish with whipped cream, if desired.   Makes 8 servings

9-inch Classic Crisco® Double Crust

2 cups all-purpose flour
1 teaspoon salt
¾ CRISCO® Stick or ¾ cup CRISCO® all-vegetable shortening
5 tablespoons cold water

1 Combine flour and salt in medium bowl. Cut in shortening using pastry blender or 2 knives until flour is blended to form pea-size chunks.

2 Sprinkle with water, 1 tablespoon at a time. Toss lightly with fork until dough forms a ball.

3 Divide dough in half. Press half of dough between hands to form a 5- to 6-inch "pancake." Flour rolling surface and rolling pin lightly. Roll dough into circle. Trim circle 1 inch larger than upside-down pie plate. Carefully remove trimmed dough. Set aside to reroll and use for pastry cutout garnish, if desired. Repeat with remaining half of dough.

Makes 2 (9-inch) crusts

- Make It Special -
To add interest to a double-crust fruit pie, cut shapes out of the top crust with hors d'oeuvre cutters or small cookie cutters before placing top crust on the pie.

Amaretto Coconut Cream Pie

¼ cup flaked coconut
1 container (8 ounces) thawed nondairy whipped topping, divided
1 container (8 ounces) coconut-cream-flavored or vanilla-flavored yogurt
¼ cup amaretto liqueur
1 package (4-serving size) instant coconut pudding and pie filling mix
1 (9-inch) prepared graham cracker pie crust
Fresh strawberries (optional)

Preheat oven to 350°F. To toast coconut, place coconut on baking sheet. Bake 4 to 5 minutes or until golden brown, stirring frequently. Cool completely.

Place 2 cups whipped topping, yogurt and amaretto in large bowl. Add pudding mix. Beat with wire whisk or electric mixer on low speed, 1 to 2 minutes or until thickened.

Pour pudding mixture into crust; spread remaining whipped topping over filling. Sprinkle with toasted coconut. Garnish with fresh strawberries, if desired. Refrigerate.
Makes 8 servings

Apple Cranberry Pie

1 package (8 ounces) PHILADELPHIA BRAND® Cream Cheese, softened
½ cup firmly packed brown sugar, divided
1 egg
1 unbaked pastry shell (9-inch)
2 cups sliced peeled apples
½ cup halved cranberries
1 teaspoon ground cinnamon, divided
⅓ cup flour
⅓ cup old-fashioned or quick-cooking oats, uncooked
¼ cup (½ stick) butter or margarine
¼ cup chopped nuts

MIX cream cheese and ¼ cup of the sugar with electric mixer on medium speed until well blended. Blend in egg. Pour into pastry shell.

TOSS apples, cranberries and ½ teaspoon of the cinnamon. Spoon over cream cheese mixture.

MIX flour, oats, remaining ¼ cup sugar and ½ teaspoon cinnamon; cut in butter until mixture resembles coarse crumbs. Stir in nuts. Spoon over fruit mixture.

BAKE at 375°F for 40 to 45 minutes or until lightly browned.
Makes 8 to 10 servings

Prep time: 15 minutes
Bake time: 45 minutes

Amaretto Coconut Cream Pie

Classic Pecan Pie

3 eggs
1 cup sugar
1 cup KARO® Light or Dark
    Corn Syrup
2 tablespoons MAZOLA®
    Margarine or butter,
    melted
1 teaspoon vanilla
1½ cups pecans
    Easy-As-Pie Crust (recipe
    follows) or 1 (9-inch) frozen
    deep-dish pie crust*

To use prepared frozen pie crust: Do not thaw. Preheat oven and cookie sheet. Pour filling into frozen crust. Bake on cookie sheet. (Insulated cookie sheets are not recommended.)

1 Preheat oven to 350°F.

2 In medium bowl with fork, beat eggs slightly. Add sugar, corn syrup, margarine and vanilla; stir until well blended. Stir in pecans. Pour into pie crust.

3 Bake 50 to 55 minutes or until knife inserted halfway between center and edge comes out clean. Cool on wire rack.

Makes 8 servings

Prep time: 6 minutes
Bake time: 50 minutes, plus cooling

Almond Amaretto Pie: *Substitute 1 cup sliced almonds for pecans. Add 2 tablespoons almond-flavored liqueur and ½ teaspoon almond extract to filling.*

Butterscotch Pecan Pie: *Omit margarine; add ¼ cup heavy or whipping cream to filling.*

Chocolate Chip Walnut Pie: *Substitute 1 cup walnuts, coarsely chopped, for pecans. Sprinkle ½ cup semisweet chocolate chips over bottom pie crust. Carefully pour filling into pie crust.*

Easy-As-Pie Crust

1¼ cups unsifted all-purpose
    flour
⅛ teaspoon salt
½ cup (1 stick) MAZOLA®
    Margarine
2 to 3 tablespoons cold water

1 In medium bowl combine flour and salt. With pastry blender or 2 knives, cut in margarine until mixture resembles fine crumbs.

2 Sprinkle water over mixture while tossing to blend well. Press dough firmly into ball.

3 On lightly floured surface, roll into 12-inch circle. Fit loosely into 9-inch pie plate. Trim and flute edge. Fill and bake according to recipe.   Makes single pie crust

Baked Pie Shell: *Preheat oven to 450°F. Pierce pie crust thoroughly with fork. Bake 12 to 15 minutes or until light golden brown.*

Top to bottom: Almond Amaretto Pie,
Classic Pecan Pie

Homemade Quick Breads

Banana Nut Bread

- ½ **cup granulated sugar**
- 2 **tablespoons brown sugar**
- 5 **tablespoons margarine**
- 1⅓ **cups mashed ripe bananas (2 medium)**
- 1 **egg**
- 2 **egg whites**
- 2½ **cups all-purpose flour**
- 1 **teaspoon baking soda**
- ½ **teaspoon salt**
- ⅓ **cup walnuts**

Preheat oven to 375°F. Spray large loaf pan with nonstick cooking spray; set aside.

Beat sugars and margarine in large bowl with electric mixer until light and fluffy. Add bananas, egg and egg whites. Sift flour, baking soda and salt into medium bowl; add to banana mixture. Stir in walnuts. Pour into prepared pan.

Bake 1 hour or until toothpick inserted into center comes out clean. Remove from pan; cool on wire rack 10 minutes. Serve warm or cool completely.

Makes 1 loaf (16 servings)

*Favorite recipe from **The Sugar Association, Inc.***

Banana Nut Bread

Glazed Strawberry Lemon Streusel Muffins

Lemon Streusel Topping (recipe follows)
Lemony Glaze (recipe follows)
1½ **cups all-purpose flour**
½ **cup sugar**
2 **teaspoons baking powder**
1 **teaspoon ground cinnamon**
¼ **teaspoon salt**
½ **cup milk**
½ **cup (1 stick) butter or margarine, melted**
1 **egg**
1½ **cups fresh strawberries, chopped**
1 **teaspoon grated lemon peel**

Preheat oven to 375°F. Line 12 (2½-inch) muffin cups with liners. Prepare Lemon Streusel Topping and Lemony Glaze; set aside. Combine flour, sugar, baking powder, cinnamon and salt in large bowl. Combine milk, butter and egg in small bowl until well blended. Stir into flour mixture just until moistened. Fold in strawberries and lemon peel. Spoon evenly into prepared muffin cups. Sprinkle Lemon Streusel Topping evenly over tops of muffins. Bake 20 to 25 minutes or until toothpick inserted in center comes out clean. Remove from pan. Cool on wire rack 10 minutes. Drizzle with Lemony Glaze. Serve warm or cool completely.   Makes 12 muffins

Lemon Streusel Topping: Combine ¼ cup chopped pecans, ¼ cup packed brown sugar, 2 tablespoons all-purpose flour, ½ teaspoon ground cinnamon and ½ teaspoon grated lemon peel in medium bowl. Add 1 tablespoon melted butter or margarine, stirring until crumbly.

Lemony Glaze: Combine ½ cup powdered sugar and 1 tablespoon fresh lemon juice in small bowl, stirring until smooth.

Plantation Peanut Bread

2 **cups all-purpose flour**
1 **cup sugar**
2 **teaspoons baking powder**
1 **teaspoon salt**
1 **cup PETER PAN® Chunky Peanut Butter**
1 **egg**
1 **cup milk**

In large bowl, combine flour, sugar, baking powder and salt. Add peanut butter; mix until crumbly. In small bowl, combine egg and milk; mix well. Add to peanut butter mixture; mix until moistened. Pour batter into greased 9×5×3-inch loaf pan. Bake in 325°F oven for 50 minutes or until toothpick inserted in center comes out clean. Cool on wire rack for 10 minutes; remove from pan and let cool completely.
      Makes 1 loaf

Smucker's® Orange Marmalade Bread

2½ cups all-purpose flour
1 tablespoon baking powder
1 teaspoon salt
½ cup honey
2 tablespoons butter, softened
3 eggs, beaten
1 (12-ounce) jar SMUCKER'S® Orange Marmalade
1 tablespoon grated orange peel
1 cup finely chopped pecans (optional)

Preheat oven to 350°F. Combine flour, baking powder and salt in bowl.

Beat honey, butter and eggs in separate bowl until smooth. Stir in Smucker's® Orange Marmalade and orange peel, mixing well.

Add flour mixture, stirring until well blended. Add nuts. Bake in greased loaf pan for 1 hour. Cool for 10 minutes. Let loaf cool completely for easier slicing.

Makes 10 servings

Prep time: 10 minutes
Cook time: 1 hour

Glazed Strawberry Lemon Streusel Muffins

Apple Ring Coffee Cake

3 cups all-purpose flour
1 teaspoon baking soda
1 teaspoon salt
1 teaspoon ground cinnamon
1 cup chopped walnuts
1½ cups granulated sugar
1 cup vegetable oil
2 eggs
2 teaspoons vanilla
2 cups peeled, chopped tart
    apples
    Powdered sugar, for garnish

Preheat oven to 325°F. Grease 10-inch tube pan; set aside.

Sift together flour, baking soda, salt and cinnamon into large bowl. Stir in walnuts. Combine granulated sugar, oil, eggs and vanilla in medium bowl. Stir in apples. Stir into flour mixture just until moistened. Spoon batter into prepared pan, spreading evenly.

Bake 1 hour or until toothpick inserted in center comes out clean. Cool cake in pan on wire rack 10 minutes. Remove from pan; cool completely on wire rack. Sprinkle powdered sugar over cake.

Makes 12 servings

- Sell It -

Wrap loaves of quick breads and coffee cakes in plastic wrap and tie with a fancy ribbon or raffia.

Banana Blueberry Muffins

2 extra-ripe, medium DOLE®
    Bananas, peeled
6 tablespoons margarine
6 tablespoons brown sugar
1 egg
1½ cups all-purpose flour
½ teaspoon baking powder
½ teaspoon baking soda
½ teaspoon salt
½ teaspoon grated lemon peel
1 cup frozen blueberries,
    rinsed, drained

• Purée bananas in blender (1 cup).

• Beat margarine and sugar until light and fluffy. Mix in bananas and egg.

• Combine flour, baking powder, baking soda, salt and lemon peel. Blend into mixture just until moistened. Fold in blueberries.

• Line 6 large muffin cups with paper liners. Coat lightly with vegetable spray. Divide batter evenly.

• Bake in 375°F oven 20 to 25 minutes.   Makes 6 muffins

Prep time: 20 minutes
Bake time: 25 minutes

Apple Ring Coffee Cake

Pumpkin Harvest Bread

Pumpkin Harvest Bread

1½ cups all-purpose flour
½ cup ALBERS® Yellow Corn Meal
2 teaspoons ground cinnamon
1½ teaspoons baking powder
1 teaspoon baking soda
½ teaspoon ground nutmeg
¼ teaspoon salt
1 cup LIBBY'S® Solid Pack Pumpkin
2 eggs
½ cup granulated sugar
½ cup packed brown sugar
¼ cup vegetable oil
¼ cup applesauce
½ cup raisins

COMBINE flour, corn meal, cinnamon, baking powder, baking soda, nutmeg and salt in medium bowl. Beat pumpkin, eggs, granulated sugar, brown sugar, oil and applesauce in large mixer bowl until combined. Beat in flour mixture just until blended. Stir in raisins. Spoon into greased, floured 9×5-inch loaf pan.

BAKE in preheated 350°F. oven for 50 to 55 minutes or until wooden pick inserted in center comes out clean. Cool in pan on wire rack for 5 to 10 minutes. Remove to wire rack to cool completely.

Makes 18 servings

Blueberry Coffee Cake

2⅓ cups all-purpose flour
1⅓ cups plus 2 tablespoons
    granulated sugar, divided
½ teaspoon salt
¾ CRISCO® Stick or ¾ cup
    CRISCO® all-vegetable
    shortening
¾ cup milk
3 eggs
2 teaspoons baking powder
1 teaspoon vanilla
1 cup ricotta cheese
1 tablespoon finely grated fresh
    lemon peel
1 cup fresh or frozen
    blueberries
½ cup chopped walnuts
⅓ cup packed brown sugar
1 teaspoon cinnamon
    Confectioners Sugar Icing
    (recipe follows)

1 **Preheat** oven to 350°F. **Grease** 13×9×2-inch baking pan; set aside.

2 **Combine** flour, *1⅓ cups* granulated sugar and salt in bowl. **Cut in** shortening until crumbly. **Reserve** *1 cup* mixture for topping. **Add** milk, 2 eggs, baking powder and vanilla to remaining mixture. **Beat** at medium speed 2 minutes, scraping bowl. **Spread** in prepared pan.

3 **Combine** remaining 2 tablespoons sugar, remaining egg, ricotta cheese and lemon peel in bowl. **Mix** well. **Sprinkle** blueberries over batter in the pan.

Spoon cheese mixture over berries. **Spread** cheese mixture gently and evenly.

4 **Mix** reserved crumb mixture, nuts, brown sugar and cinnamon. **Sprinkle** over cake. **Bake** at 350°F about 45 minutes or until toothpick inserted in center comes out clean. **Cool** slightly. **Drizzle** with Confectioners Sugar Icing.   Makes 12 servings

Confectioners Sugar Icing:
Combine 1 cup confectioners sugar, 1 tablespoon milk, orange juice or orange-flavored liqueur and ¼ teaspoon vanilla in small bowl. Stir in additional milk, 1 teaspoon at a time, until icing is of desired drizzling consistency. Makes about ½ cup.

- Make It Special -

A quick drizzle of powdered sugar glaze adds a festive note to any coffee cake or quick bread loaf and gives it a professional look (see page 9 for directions). Be sure to wait until the bread has cooled before adding the glaze or it will be absorbed into the bread.

Snacking Surprise Muffins

1½ cups all-purpose flour
½ cup sugar
1 cup fresh or frozen
    blueberries
2½ teaspoons baking powder
1 teaspoon ground cinnamon
¼ teaspoon salt
1 egg, beaten
⅔ cup buttermilk
¼ cup (½ stick) butter or
    margarine, melted
3 tablespoons peach preserves

TOPPING

1 tablespoon sugar
¼ teaspoon ground cinnamon

1 Preheat oven to 400°F. Line 12 medium muffin cups with paper liners; set aside.

2 Combine flour, ½ cup sugar, blueberries, baking powder, 1 teaspoon cinnamon and salt in medium bowl. Combine egg, buttermilk and butter in small bowl. Add to flour mixture; mix just until moistened.

3 Spoon about 1 tablespoon batter into each muffin cup. Drop a scant teaspoonful of preserves into center of batter in each cup; top with remaining batter.

4 Combine 1 tablespoon sugar and ¼ teaspoon cinnamon in small bowl; sprinkle evenly over batter.

5 Bake 18 to 20 minutes or until lightly browned. Remove muffins to wire rack to cool completely.   Makes 12 muffins

Oreo® Muffins

1¾ cups all-purpose flour
½ cup sugar
1 tablespoon DAVIS® Baking
    Powder
½ teaspoon salt
¾ cup milk
⅓ cup sour cream
1 egg
¼ cup margarine, melted
20 OREO® Chocolate Sandwich
    Cookies, coarsely chopped

In medium bowl, combine flour, sugar, baking powder and salt; set aside.

In small bowl, combine milk, sour cream and egg; stir into flour mixture with margarine until just blended. Gently stir in cookies. Spoon batter into 12 greased 2½-inch muffin cups.

Bake at 400°F for 20 to 25 minutes or until toothpick inserted in center comes out clean. Remove from pan; cool on wire rack. Serve warm or cold.

Makes 1 dozen muffins

Snacking Surprise Muffins

Mocha Walnut Crunch Coffeecake

COFFEECAKE
- 1 (16-ounce) package hot roll mix
- 1 cup QUAKER® Oats (Quick or Old Fashioned), uncooked
- ¼ teaspoon salt (optional)
- ¾ cup milk
- ½ cup (1 stick) margarine or butter
- ½ cup sugar
- 3 eggs, at room temperature
- ½ cup semi-sweet chocolate pieces

TOPPING
- ½ cup all-purpose flour
- ½ cup sugar
- ¼ cup QUAKER® Oats (Quick or Old Fashioned), uncooked
- 1 tablespoon instant coffee granules or espresso powder
- ½ cup (1 stick) margarine or butter, chilled
- ½ cup semi-sweet chocolate pieces
- ½ cup chopped walnuts

Grease 12-cup Bundt pan or 10-inch tube pan.

For coffeecake, in large mixing bowl, combine hot roll mix (including yeast packet), oats and salt; mix well. In small saucepan, heat milk and margarine over low heat until margarine is melted; remove from heat. Stir in sugar; cool mixture to 120°F to 130°F. Add to oat mixture; add eggs. Beat at low speed of electric mixer until well blended. Stir in chocolate pieces. Spoon into prepared pan.

For topping, combine flour, sugar, oats and coffee granules; cut in margarine until mixture is crumbly. Stir in chocolate pieces and nuts. Sprinkle evenly over top of dough. Cover loosely with plastic wrap. Let rise in warm place 30 to 40 minutes or until nearly double in size.

Heat oven to 350°F. Bake, uncovered, 45 to 50 minutes or until wooden pick inserted in center comes out clean. Cool in pan 10 minutes. Remove from pan, topping side up, onto wire rack. Cool completely. Store tightly covered.   Makes 16 servings

Note: *If hot roll mix is not available, combine 3 cups all-purpose flour, two ¼-ounce packages quick-rising yeast and 1½ teaspoons salt; mix well. Continue as recipe directs.*

- Make It Special -
Coarse sugar (also called decorating or crystal sugar) adds a jazzy topping to sweet muffins. Just dip the tops of hot muffins into a little melted butter or margarine, then into the coarse sugar.

Mocha Walnut Crunch Coffeecake

Raisin Zucchini Muffins

1 egg
¾ cup nonfat milk
½ cup brown sugar, packed
⅓ cup vegetable oil
1½ cups shredded zucchini
2 tablespoons grated orange peel
2 cups all-purpose flour
1 tablespoon baking powder
¼ teaspoon *each* salt, cinnamon, ginger, nutmeg
⅛ teaspoon ground cloves
1 cup DOLE® Raisins
½ cup DOLE® Chopped Almonds, toasted

• Beat egg, milk, brown sugar and oil. Stir in zucchini and orange peel.

• Combine remaining ingredients. Stir into zucchini mixture just until moistened.

• Spoon into 12 muffin cups coated with cooking spray. Bake in 375°F oven 25 minutes. Serve warm.

Makes 12 muffins

Prep time: 20 minutes
Bake time: 25 minutes

Lemon Poppy Seed Muffins

3 cups all-purpose flour
1 cup sugar
3 tablespoons poppy seeds
1 tablespoon grated lemon peel
2 teaspoons baking powder
1 teaspoon baking soda
½ teaspoon salt
1 container (16 ounces) plain
   low-fat yogurt
½ cup fresh lemon juice
¼ cup vegetable oil
2 eggs, beaten
1½ teaspoons vanilla

Preheat oven to 400°F. Grease 12 (3½-inch) large muffin cups; set aside.

Combine flour, sugar, poppy seeds, lemon peel, baking powder, baking soda and salt in large bowl. Combine yogurt, lemon juice, oil, eggs and vanilla in small bowl until well blended. Stir into flour mixture just until moistened. Spoon into prepared muffin cups, filling two-thirds full.

Bake 25 to 30 minutes or until toothpick inserted in center comes out clean. Cool in pans on wire racks 5 minutes. Remove from pans; cool on wire racks 10 minutes. Serve warm or cool completely.

Makes 12 jumbo muffins

The Original Kellogg's All-Bran Muffin™

1¼ cups all-purpose flour
½ cup sugar
1 tablespoon baking powder
¼ teaspoon salt
2 cups KELLOGG'S®
   ALL-BRAN® Cereal
1¼ cups low-fat milk
1 egg
¼ cup vegetable oil
   Vegetable cooking spray

1 Stir together flour, sugar, baking powder and salt. Set aside.

2 In large mixing bowl, combine Kellogg's® All-Bran® cereal and milk. Let stand about 5 minutes or until cereal softens. Add egg and oil. Beat well. Add flour mixture, stirring only until combined. Portion batter evenly into twelve 2½-inch muffin pan cups coated with cooking spray.

3 Bake at 400°F about 20 minutes or until lightly browned. Serve warm.

Makes 12 muffins

For muffins with reduced calories, fat and cholesterol: *Use 2 tablespoons sugar, 2 tablespoons oil, replace low-fat milk with 1¼ cups skim milk, and substitute 2 egg whites for 1 egg. Prepare and bake as directed.*

Lemon Poppy Seed Muffins

Quick Tricks with Mixes

Peanut Butter Bars

**1 package DUNCAN HINES®
   Peanut Butter Cookie Mix**
2 egg whites
**¼ cup CRISCO® Oil or
   CRISCO® PURITAN®
   Canola Oil**
½ cup chopped peanuts
1 cup confectioners sugar
2 tablespoons water
½ teaspoon vanilla extract

1 Preheat oven to 350°F.

2 Combine cookie mix, peanut butter packet from Mix, egg whites and oil in large bowl. Stir until thoroughly blended. Press into ungreased 13×9×2-inch pan. Sprinkle peanuts over dough. Press lightly.

3 Bake at 350°F for 18 to 20 minutes or until golden brown. Cool completely. Combine confectioners sugar, water and vanilla extract in small bowl. Stir until blended. Drizzle glaze over top. Cut into bars.

Makes 24 bars

- Make It Special -
A dusting of powdered sugar doesn't travel well on most desserts because the moisture in the baked goods liquefies the sugar. Dust brownies and cakes with powdered sugar at the last minute; just fill a salt shaker to take along to the bake sale—it's quick and convenient.

Peanut Butter Bars

Orange Honey Cake

1 package DUNCAN HINES®
    Moist Deluxe Butter Recipe
    Golden Cake Mix
4 eggs
1 cup orange juice, divided
½ cup butter or margarine,
    softened
2 tablespoons grated orange
    peel, divided (2 oranges)
¼ cup honey
    Orange peel strips or orange
    slices, for garnish (optional)
    Mint leaves (optional)

1 Preheat oven to 375°F. Grease and flour 10-inch Bundt or tube pan.

2 Place cake mix, eggs, ¾ cup orange juice and butter in large bowl. Reserve ½ teaspoon grated orange peel; set aside. Add remaining grated orange peel to cake mixture. Beat at low speed with electric mixer until moistened. Beat at medium speed for 4 minutes. Pour into pan. Bake at 375°F for 45 to 50 minutes or until toothpick inserted in center comes out clean. Cool in pan 25 minutes. Invert onto serving plate.

3 Combine honey, remaining ¼ cup orange juice and reserved ½ teaspoon orange peel in small bowl. Pour gradually over warm cake. Cool completely. Garnish with orange peel strips and mint leaves, if desired.

Makes 12 to 16 servings

Cream-Filled Banana Cupcakes

Cream Cheese Filling (recipe
    follows)
1 package (18.5 ounces) banana
    cake mix (with pudding in
    the mix)
¾ cup finely chopped nuts
2 tablespoons sugar

Prepare Cream Cheese Filling; set aside. Heat oven to 350°F. Prepare cake batter according to package directions. Fill paper-lined muffin cups (2½ inches in diameter) ½ full with batter. Spoon about 1 teaspoonful filling into center of each cupcake. Combine nuts and sugar; sprinkle about 1 teaspoonful over top of each cupcake. Bake 20 minutes or until wooden pick inserted in cake portion comes out clean. Cool on wire racks.

Makes about 3 dozen
cupcakes

Cream Cheese Filling

1 package (8 ounces) cream
    cheese, softened
⅓ cup sugar
1 egg
1 cup HERSHEY'S MINI
    CHIPS® Semi-Sweet
    Chocolate

In small bowl combine cream cheese, sugar and egg; beat until smooth. Stir in small chocolate chips.

Orange Honey Cake

Chewy Chocolate Cookies

1 package (2-layer size)
    chocolate cake mix
2 eggs
1 cup MIRACLE WHIP® or
    MIRACLE WHIP® LIGHT
    Salad Dressing
1 cup BAKER'S® Semi-Sweet
    Real Chocolate Chips
½ cup chopped walnuts

MIX cake mix, eggs and dressing in large bowl with electric mixer on medium speed until blended. Stir in remaining ingredients. Drop by rounded teaspoonfuls onto greased cookie sheets.

BAKE at 350°F for 10 to 12 minutes or until edges are lightly browned.

Makes 4 dozen cookies

Prep time: 10 minutes
Bake time: 12 minutes

Apricot Date Mini-Loaves

Apricot Date Mini-Loaves

1 package DUNCAN HINES®
   Cinnamon Muffin Mix
½ teaspoon baking powder
2 egg whites
⅔ cup water
½ cup chopped dried apricots
½ cup chopped dates

1 Preheat oven to 350°F. Grease four 5⅜×2⅝×1⅞-inch mini-loaf pans.

2 Combine muffin mix and baking powder in large bowl. Break up any lumps. Add egg whites, water, apricots and dates. Stir until well blended, about 50 strokes.

3 Knead swirl packet from Mix for 10 seconds before opening. Cut off one end of swirl packet. Squeeze contents onto batter. Swirl into batter with knife or spatula, folding from bottom of bowl to get an even swirl. *Do not completely mix into batter.* Divide batter evenly into pans. Sprinkle with topping packet from Mix.

4 Bake at 350°F for 30 to 35 minutes or until toothpick inserted in center comes out clean. Cool 15 minutes. Loosen loaves from pans. Lift out with knife. Cool completely.

Makes 4 mini-loaves

Tip: *This recipe may also be baked in greased 8½×4½×2½-inch loaf pan at 350°F for 55 to 60 minutes*

or until toothpick inserted in center comes out clean. Cool 10 minutes before removing loaf from pan.

Pumpkin Crunch Cake

1 package (18.25 ounces) yellow
   cake mix, *divided*
2 eggs
1⅔ cups LIBBY'S® Pumpkin Pie
   Mix
2 teaspoons pumpkin pie spice
⅓ cup flaked coconut
¼ cup chopped nuts
3 tablespoons butter or
   margarine, softened

COMBINE *3 cups* cake mix, eggs, pumpkin pie mix and pumpkin pie spice in large mixing bowl. Beat on low speed until moistened. Beat on medium speed for 2 minutes. Pour into greased 13×9-inch baking pan.

COMBINE *remaining* cake mix, coconut and nuts in small bowl; cut in butter with pastry blender or two knives until mixture is crumbly. Sprinkle over batter.

BAKE in preheated 350°F. oven for 30 to 35 minutes or until wooden pick inserted in center comes out clean. Cool in pan on wire rack. Makes 20 servings

Chocolate Chip Lollipops

1 package DUNCAN HINES®
Chocolate Chip Cookie Mix
1 egg
⅓ cup CRISCO® Oil or
CRISCO® PURITAN®
Canola Oil
2 tablespoons water
Flat ice cream sticks
Assorted decors

1 Preheat oven to 375°F.

2 Combine cookie mix, egg, oil and water in large bowl. Stir until thoroughly blended. Shape dough into 32 (1-inch) balls. Place balls 3 inches apart on ungreased baking sheets. Push ice cream stick into center of each ball. Flatten dough ball with hand to form round lollipop. Decorate by pressing decors onto dough. Bake at 375°F for 8 to 9 minutes or until light golden brown. Cool 1 minute on baking sheets. Remove to cooling racks. Cool completely. Store in airtight container.

Makes 2½ to 3 dozen cookies

Tip: *For best results, use shiny baking sheets for baking cookies. Dark baking sheets cause cookie bottoms to become too brown.*

Marbled Chocolate Sour Cream Cake

1 cup (6 ounces) NESTLÉ®
TOLL HOUSE® Semi-
Sweet Chocolate Morsels
1 package (18.5 ounces) yellow
cake mix
4 eggs
¾ cup sour cream
½ cup vegetable oil
¼ cup water
¼ cup granulated sugar
Powdered sugar (optional)

MICROWAVE morsels in medium microwave-safe bowl on HIGH power for 1 minute; stir. Microwave at additional 10- to 20-second intervals, stirring until smooth.

COMBINE cake mix, eggs, sour cream, oil, water and granulated sugar in large mixing bowl. Beat on low speed until moistened. Beat on high speed for 2 minutes.

STIR 2 cups batter into melted chocolate. Alternately spoon batters into greased 10-cup Bundt or round tube pan.

BAKE in preheated 375°F. oven for 35 to 45 minutes or until wooden pick inserted near center comes out clean. Cool in pan for 20 minutes; invert onto wire rack to cool completely. Sprinkle with powdered sugar before serving.

Makes 24 servings

Chocolate Chip Lollipops

Peanut Butter Marbled Brownies

4 ounces cream cheese, softened
½ cup peanut butter
2 tablespoons sugar
1 egg
1 package (20 to 22 ounces) brownie mix plus ingredients to prepare mix
¾ cup lightly salted cocktail peanuts

Preheat oven to 350°F. Lightly grease 13×9-inch baking pan; set aside. Beat cream cheese, peanut butter, sugar and egg in medium bowl with electric mixer at medium speed until blended; set aside.

Prepare brownie mix according to package directions. Spread brownie mixture evenly in prepared pan. Spoon peanut butter mixture in dollops over brownie mixture. Swirl peanut butter mixture into brownie mixture with tip of knife. Sprinkle peanuts on top; lightly press peanuts down.

Bake 30 to 35 minutes or until toothpick inserted into center comes out almost clean. *Do not overbake.* Cool brownies completely in pan on wire rack; cut into 2-inch squares. Store tightly covered at room temperature or freeze up to 3 months.

Makes 24 brownies

Easy Carrot Cake

1¼ cups MIRACLE WHIP® Salad Dressing
1 two-layer yellow cake mix
4 eggs
¼ cup cold water
2 teaspoons ground cinnamon
2 cups finely shredded carrots
½ cup chopped walnuts
1 (16-ounce) container ready-to-spread cream cheese frosting

BEAT salad dressing, cake mix, eggs, water and cinnamon in large bowl with electric mixer at medium speed until well blended. Stir in carrots and walnuts. Pour batter into greased 13×9-inch baking pan.

BAKE at 350°F for 30 to 35 minutes or until wooden toothpick inserted in center comes out clean. Cool completely. Spread cake with frosting. Garnish as desired.

Makes 12 servings

Prep time: 15 minutes
Bake time: 35 minutes

- Sell It -

To share a recipe, print it on a recipe card, punch a hole in the corner and tie on a ribbon or just attach it to the box or bag of baked goods.

Peanut Butter Marbled Brownies

German Chocolate Muffins

German Chocolate Topping (recipe follows)
1 package (18¼ ounces) pudding-included German chocolate cake mix

Preheat oven to 400°F. Grease 12 (3½-inch) large muffin cups; set aside. Prepare German Chocolate Topping; set aside.

Prepare cake mix according to package directions, *reducing* water by ¼ cup. Spoon into prepared muffin cups, filling half full. Sprinkle German Chocolate Topping evenly over tops of muffins.

Bake 20 to 25 minutes or until toothpick inserted in center comes out clean. Cool in pan on wire rack 5 minutes. Remove from pan. Cool on wire rack 10 minutes. Serve warm or cool completely.

Makes 12 jumbo muffins

German Chocolate Topping:
Combine 3 tablespoons *each* chopped pecans, flaked coconut and packed brown sugar in small bowl until well blended.

Chocolate Caramel Nut Bars

1 package (18¼ ounces) devil's food cake mix
¾ cup (1½ sticks) butter or margarine, melted
½ cup milk, divided
60 vanilla caramels
1 cup cashew pieces, coarsely chopped
1 cup semisweet chocolate chips

Preheat oven to 350°F. Grease 13×9-inch baking pan. Combine cake mix, butter and ¼ cup milk in medium bowl; mix well. Press half of batter onto bottom of prepared pan.

Bake 7 to 8 minutes. Remove from oven. Meanwhile, combine caramels and remaining ¼ cup milk in heavy medium saucepan. Cook over low heat, stirring often, about 5 minutes or until caramels are melted and mixture is smooth.

Pour melted caramel mixture over partially baked crust. Combine cashews and chocolate chips; sprinkle over caramel mixture.

Drop spoonfuls of remaining batter evenly over nut mixture. Return pan to oven; bake 18 to 20 minutes more or until top cake layer springs back when lightly touched. (Caramel center will be soft.) Cool on wire racks.

Makes about 48 bars

German Chocolate Muffins

Acknowledgments

The publishers would like to thank the companies and organizations listed below for the use of their recipes in this publication.

Best Foods Division, CPC International Inc.

Blue Diamond Growers

Cherry Marketing Institute, Inc.

Dole Food Company, Inc.

Hershey Foods Corporation

Kellogg Company

Kraft Foods, Inc.

M&M/MARS

Nabisco, Inc.

Nestlé USA

The Procter & Gamble Company

Quaker® Kitchens

The J.M. Smucker Company

Sunkist Growers

Wesson/Peter Pan Foods Company

Index

Almond Amaretto Pie, 64
Almonds
  Almond Amaretto Pie, 64
  Almond Coconut Butter
    Cake, 52
  Almond Toffee Squares,
    29
  Banana Chocolate Chip
    Bars, 29
  Double Almond Butter
    Cookies, 22
  Raisin Zucchini Muffins,
    77
Almond Toffee Squares, 29
Amaretto Coconut Cream
  Pie, 62
Apples
  Apple Cranberry Pie, 62
  Apple Ring Coffee Cake,
    70
  Apple Upside-Down
    Cake, 54
  New York Apple Maple
    Cream Pie, 58
Apricot Date Mini-Loaves,
  85

Baking Bits
  Crispy Oat Drops, 23
  Hershey®s Soft & Chewy
    Cookies, 17
  Rainbow Blondies, 35
  Reese's® Bits Blondies, 30
Bananas
  Banana Blueberry
    Muffins, 70
  Banana Chocolate Chip
    Bars, 29
  Banana Nut Bread, 66
  Cream-Filled Banana
    Cupcakes, 82
Blueberries
  Banana Blueberry
    Muffins, 70
  Banana Cake, 48
  Blueberry Coffee Cake, 73
  Snacking Surprise
    Muffins, 74
Butterscotch Pecan Pie, 64

Caramels
  Caramel-Layered
    Brownies, 38
  Chocolate Caramel Nut
    Bars, 90
Cashews: Chocolate Caramel
    Nut Bars, 90
Cherries: Traditional Cherry
    Pie, 58
Chewy Chocolate Cookies,
  84
Chocolate, Baking (*see also*
    Chocolate Chips; Cocoa)
  Almond Toffee Squares, 29
  Caramel-Layered
    Brownies, 38
  Chocolate Curls, 8
  Chocolate-Dipped
    Strawberries, 9
  Chocolate Drizzle, 8
  Chocolate Leaves, 8
  Chocolate Marble
    Cheesecake, 45
  Chocolate New York
    Cheesecake, 50
  Extra Moist & Chunky
    Brownies, 37
  melting directions, 7
  One-Bowl™ Brownies, 34
  Oreo® Pecan Fudge Pie,
    61
  Peanut Butter Swirl
    Brownies, 34
  Rocky Road Brownies, 34
Chocolate Brownie Frosting,
  30
Chocolate Caramel Nut
  Bars, 90
Chocolate Cheesecake
  Cupcakes, 42
Chocolate Chips
  Banana Chocolate Chip
    Bars, 29
  Caramel-Layered
    Brownies, 38
  Chewy Chocolate
    Cookies, 84
  Chocolate Caramel Nut
    Bars, 90

Chocolate Cheesecake
  Cupcakes, 42
Chocolate Chip Lollipops,
  86
Chocolate Chip Walnut
  Pie, 64
Chocolate Chocolate
  Cookies, 17
Chocolate Curls, 8
Chocolate-Dipped
  Strawberries, 9
Chocolate Drizzle, 8
Chocolate Leaves, 8
Cream Cheese Filling, 82
Heavenly Oat Bars, 33
Hershey®s Milk Chocolate
  Chip Giant Cookies, 24
Hershey®s Soft & Chewy
  Cookies, 17
Marbled Chocolate Sour
  Cream Cake, 86
Mini Morsel Pound Cake, 40
Mocha Walnut Crunch
  Coffeecake, 76
Moist and Minty
  Brownies, 32
No-Bake Peanutty
  Cookies, 14
No-Fuss Bar Cookies, 38
Peanut Chocolate Surprise
  Pie, 60
Polka Dot Pumpkin
  Cupcakes, 52
Raspberry Coconut Layer
  Bars, 33
Rocky Road Brownies, 32,
  34
Chocolate Marble
  Cheesecake, 45
Chocolate New York
  Cheesecake, 50
Classic Pecan Pie, 64
Cocoa
  Chocolate Brownie
    Frosting, 30
  Chocolate Chocolate
    Cookies, 17
  Deep Dark Chocolate
    Cake, 44

Double Chocolate Peanut Cookies made with Snickers® Bars, 24
Mississippi Nilla® Mud Cake, 46
One-Bowl Buttercream Frosting, 44
Rocky Road Brownies, 32
Coconut
Almond Coconut Butter Cake, 52
Almond Toffee Squares, 29
Amaretto Coconut Cream Pie, 62
Coconut Cupcakes, 45
Crispy Oat Drops, 23
No-Fuss Bar Cookies, 38
Peachy Oatmeal Bars, 36
Pumpkin Crunch Cake, 85
Raspberry Coconut Layer Bars, 33
tinting directions, 9
toasting directions, 9
Confectioners Sugar Icing, 73
Cranberries
Apple Cranberry Pie, 62
Harvest Pumpkin Cookies, 22
Cream Cheese
Apple Cranberry Pie, 62
Chocolate Cheesecake Cupcakes, 42
Chocolate Marble Cheesecake, 45
Chocolate New York Cheesecake, 50
Cream Cheese Filling, 82
Cream-Filled Banana Cupcakes, 82
Extra Moist & Chunky Brownies, 37
New York Cheesecake, 50
Peanut Butter Marbled Brownies, 88
Polka Dot Pumpkin Cupcakes, 52
Praline Bars, 26
Crispy Oat Drops, 23

Deep Dark Chocolate Cake, 44
Double Almond Butter Cookies, 22
Double Chocolate Peanut Cookies made with Snickers® Bars, 24

Easy-As-Pie Crust, 64
Easy Carrot Cake, 88
Extra Moist & Chunky Brownies, 37

Fillings
Cream Cheese Filling, 82
Fruit Filling, 53
Fresh Lemon Meringue Pie, 56
Fresh Orange Cookies, 17
Frostings & Icings (*see also* **Glazes; Toppings**)
Chocolate Brownie Frosting, 30
Confectioners Sugar Icing, 73
Frosting, 48
One-Bowl Buttercream Frosting, 44
Strawberry Frosting, 53
Fruit Filling, 53

German Chocolate Muffins, 90
Glazed Strawberry Lemon Streusel Muffins, 68
Glazes
Lemony Glaze, 68
Orange Glaze, 17
Powdered Sugar Glaze, 9

Harvest Pumpkin Cookies, 22
Heavenly Oat Bars, 33
Hershey®s Milk Chocolate Chip Giant Cookies, 24
Hershey®s Soft & Chewy Cookies, 17

Lemon
Fresh Lemon Meringue Pie, 56
Glazed Strawberry Lemon Streusel Muffins, 68
Lemon Poppy Seed Cupcakes, 50

Lemon Poppy Seed Muffins, 78
Lemon Streusel Topping, 68
Lemony Glaze, 68

Marbled Chocolate Sour Cream Cake, 86
Marshmallows
Mississippi Nilla® Mud Cake, 46
Rocky Road Brownies, 32, 34
Mini Morsel Pound Cake, 40
Mocha Walnut Crunch Coffeecake, 76
Moist and Minty Brownies, 32
Mom's Favorite White Cake, 53

New York Apple Maple Cream Pie, 58
New York Cheesecake, 50
9-inch Classic Crisco Double Crust, 61
No-Bake Gingersnap Balls, 14
No-Bake Peanutty Cookies, 14
No-Fuss Bar Cookies, 38
Nuts (*see also specific nuts*)
Apple Crumb Squares, 37
Caramel-Layered Brownies, 38
Cream-Filled Banana Cupcakes, 82
One-Bowl™ Brownies, 34
Peanut Butter Swirl Brownies, 34
Pumpkin Crunch Cake, 85
Rocky Road Brownies, 34
toasting directions, 9

Oats
Apple Cranberry Pie, 62
Apple Crumb Squares, 37
Crispy Oat Drops, 23
Heavenly Oat Bars, 32
Mocha Walnut Crunch Coffeecake, 76
Oatmeal Raisin Cookies, 20
Peachy Oatmeal Bars, 36

One-Bowl™ Brownies, 34
One-Bowl Buttercream
 Frosting, 44
Orange
 Fresh Orange Cookies, 17
 Orange Glaze, 17
 Orange Honey Cake, 82
 Smucker's® Orange
  Marmalade Bread, 69
Oreo® Muffins, 74
Oreo® Pecan Fudge Pie, 61
Original Kellogg's All-Bran
 Muffin™, The, 78
Outrageous Brownies, 28

Peach Preserves
 Peachy Oatmeal Bars, 36
 Snacking Surprise
  Muffins, 74
Peanut Butter
 Heavenly Oat Bars, 33
 No-Bake Peanutty
  Cookies, 14
 Peanut Butter Bears, 18
 Peanut Butter Chocolate
  Stars, 16
 Peanut Butter Crisscross
  Cookies, 16
 Peanut Butter Marbled
  Brownies, 88
 Peanut Butter Swirl
  Brownies, 34
 Plantation Peanut Bread,
  68
 Reese's® Bits Blondies, 30
Peanuts
 Peanut Butter Bars, 80
 Peanut Butter Marbled
  Brownies, 88
 Peanut Chocolate Surprise
  Pie, 60
Pecans
 Butterscotch Pecan Pie,
  64
 Classic Pecan Pie, 64
 Crispy Oat Drops, 23
 Harvest Pumpkin
  Cookies, 22
 Mississippi Nilla® Mud
  Cake, 46
 Oreo Pecan Fudge Pie,
  61
 Raspberry Pecan
  Thumbprints, 12
 Smucker's® Orange
  Marmalade Bread, 69

Pineapple: Fruit Filling, 53
Plantation Peanut Bread,
 68
Polka Dot Pumpkin
 Cupcakes, 52
Poppy Seeds
 Lemon Poppy Seed
  Cupcakes, 50
 Lemon Poppy Seed
  Muffins, 78
Powdered Sugar Glaze, 9
Praline Bars, 26
Pumpkin
 Harvest Pumpkin
  Cookies, 22
 Polka Dot Pumpkin
  Cupcakes, 52
 Pumpkin Crunch Cake,
  85
 Pumpkin Harvest Bread,
  72

Rainbow Blondies, 35
Raisins
 Oatmeal Raisin Cookies,
  20
 Pumpkin Harvest Bread,
  72
 Raisin Zucchini Muffins,
  77
Raspberry Jam
 Raspberry Coconut Layer
  Bars, 33
 Raspberry Pecan
  Thumbprints, 12
 Raspberry-Swirled
  Cheesecake, 46
 Reese's® Bits Blondies, 30
 Rocky Road Brownies, 32,
  34

Smucker's® Orange
 Marmalade Bread, 69
Snacking Surprise Muffins,
 74
Sour Cream
 Chocolate New York
  Cheesecake, 50
 Coconut Cupcakes, 45
 Marbled Chocolate Sour
  Cream Cake, 86
 New York Cheesecake, 50
Strawberries
 Chocolate-Dipped
  Strawberries, 9
 Fruit Filling, 53

Glazed Strawberry Lemon
 Streusel Muffins, 68
Mom's Favorite White
 Cake, 53
Strawberry Frosting, 53

Toppings
 Lemon Streusel Topping,
  68
 Three-Egg Meringue, 56
Traditional Cherry Pie, 58

Walnuts
 Apple Ring Coffee Cake,
  70
 Banana Cake, 48
 Banana Nut Bread, 66
 Blueberry Coffee Cake, 73
 Chewy Chocolate
  Cookies, 84
 Chocolate Chip Walnut
  Pie, 64
 Easy Carrot Cake, 88
 Fresh Orange Cookies, 17
 Mocha Walnut Crunch
  Coffeecake, 76
 No-Fuss Bar Cookies, 38
 Outrageous Brownies, 28
 Peanut Chocolate Surprise
  Pie, 60
 Rainbow Blondies, 35
 Raspberry Coconut Layer
  Bars, 33
 Rocky Road Brownies, 32
White Chocolate
 Raspberry Coconut Layer
  Bars, 33
 Strawberry Frosting, 53